48 MOUNTAINS

THE NATURE OF FEAR

BY JOHN WHITE

Cover art by
Alexandra Lewis

Cover design and illustration on cover page by
Zachary White

To my beautiful wife Anna,
and my two awesome children Zachary and Caitlyn

DISCLAIMER

This book describes the author's experience while hiking and climbing some of America's tallest state summits, and reflects his opinions and stories relating to those experiences. Some names, identifying details and photographs have been changed to protect the privacy of individuals.

CONTENTS

ACKNOWLEDGMENTS

To my very good friend Mike, There is no way I could have done most of this without you. Thank you for not only joining me on this adventure, but for also being the awesome, inspirational person you are. It has always been an honor to call you my friend.

Me & Mike on the summit of Katahdin

To my awesome writing instructor Jennie, Not only did your teaching get my story pointed in the right direction, but you personally telling me that I had a great story to tell gave me that extra push I needed to finally get it completed. Thank you so much for your guidance and inspiration.

To my wonderful cousin Bridget, I can't thank you enough for helping my novel get to that next level and encouraging me to get it published. You helped make it happen. Thank you, thank you, thank you.

PREFACE

I frequently think back on all my highpointing experiences and I wonder how much, if any, I have forgotten. Many of my stories are funny, crazy and spontaneous, while others are grueling, frustrating and even a bit frightening. My highpointing adventures have been a huge part of my life up to now, and I felt it was time to share them.

I have been sharing my mountain climbing stories with friends and family for many years now, and they always seemed to really get a kick out of them. I finally decided to write all these memories down on paper to share them with everybody. I wanted to catch them all before they disappeared forever. There are just too many memories, great memories (and some not so great) that I want to share before I lose them to time. The places, the people, the trips, the mountains, everything; what a great experience this all was.

By doing this, I also hope to be an inspiration to people to go out and perform what they might have once thought was totally impossible. Nothing is impossible if you really want it bad enough.

The flag that went to every summit with me

Chapter 1
- Kings, Part I

The strange electric buzzing noises started a few minutes into our descent from the summit. I didn't know where the sound was coming from, but it was all around me. Being approximately 35 miles from the nearest electrical source, I was very confused and curious as to what could be generating such a noise that seemed to be coming from everywhere. I stopped next to a giant rock wall to take shelter from the elements as I waited for Mike to catch up. I also took this time to try and determine where this strange, annoying sound was coming from. I was staring up the trail, watching for Mike through the snow and rain blowing furiously across the mountain when he finally came around the corner and spotted me standing there.

"Hey John! Do you hear that 'buzzing' noise?!"

"Yeah!" I yelled back through the whipping storm, relieved that I wasn't the only one hearing it, "I was just going to ask you the same question! What do you think it is?!"

"No idea!"

"Well, this is going to sound a little strange", I paused briefly, and then hesitantly added, "But the sound seems like... like it's coming from inside my head!"

Mike gave me an odd look of curiosity and skepticism, and then said, "What? How can that be if I'm hearing it too?"

"I don't know" I said with a puzzled look on my face.

We both talked about it for about a minute more, then he suggested that we get going down the mountain. We had a lot of miles ahead of us and we were burning daylight.

I was wearing a waterproof jacket as well as a baseball cap under the hood. The brim of my cap stuck out beyond the hood to shield my eyes from the non-present sun as well as the driving rain and snow. The more I thought about it, the noise actually seemed to be coming from the brim of my cap. As I was walking, I clasped the brim with my wet, glove covered fingers and the buzzing stopped. I let it go and the buzzing started up again. I stopped and turned back towards Mike.

"Mike!" I shouted. "The buzzing is in my cap!"

"What?!" Mike was way behind me again and could not hear me over the weather. I turned away from him to keep my face shielded from the torrential downpour. I kept touching the brim of my cap and letting it go again with the same exact results. I did this quite a few times and actually started to find it a little amusing.

The buzzing then started to strengthen and fluctuate in intensity. It was a deep, vibrating buzz that tickled my ears and sounded like several bumble bees on steroids were flying around in my skull. A thought started to race through my mind and my wonder immediately switched to concern and fear. I reached out and touched the towering granite wall I was walking along and the buzzing stopped. I removed my hand from the rock and it started back up again. Just then I felt the hair on my arms and on the back of my neck start to tingle. I immediately knew what was about to happen and screamed out at the top of my lungs as I dropped to the ground in absolute terror:

"LIGHTNING!"

Chapter 2
- Highpointing Beginnings

It probably began when I was a young teen back in the mid-1970s. My dad used to take my brother Chris and I on frequent weekend road trips. We seemed to do these a lot after my parents divorced. I loved these journeys tremendously because I got to see a lot of the country I had only seen on TV or read about, and it was wonderful to actually get to see it all in person. We took trips to Arizona, Utah, Nevada, and several within my home state of California. There was one trip in particular that put the mountain climbing bug into me; it was our first trip into the eastern Sierras. What a beautiful and magnificent place this was. I had never seen mountains so large before. They were enormous and reached far up into the heavens.

Dad drove us up a very steep and windy road into the Sierras to the trailhead of Mount Whitney. This place was called Whitney Portal and little did I know that I would be visiting this same spot many more times in the not too distant future. On the way up, he explained that this road had been used several times in old movies that I had never seen or even heard of; movies like High Sierra with Humphrey Bogart, and The Long, Long Trailer with Lucille Ball. Once we got to the end of the road, he stopped the car, turned off the motor, and then explained what this mountain was all about. He told us that it was the tallest mountain in the lower 48 States, that it was the tallest mountain in the country until Alaska was admitted into the Union, and a whole host of other interesting facts and data. He told us some statistics like how tall the mountain was (14,505 feet), how many miles it was to the top from where we were parked (eleven miles), and how high we were at that very moment (almost 8000 feet). He also mentioned about how he always wanted to climb Mount Whitney ever since he could remember. I asked him why he never did, and his disappointed sounding response was, "I just never got around to it."

My dad, Chris and I on one of our many road trips
(Sequoia National Park)

I started daydreaming and was not listening to a word he was saying as he described other things we could see and do in the area. I was looking up at the face of Mount Whitney and asking myself when I would be ready to climb such a magnificent mountain. It was so beautiful and yet so very intimidating at the same time.

I asked my dad if he was ever going to climb it in the future, and his response was, "I don't know... maybe someday."

"Someday," I thought to myself.

I immediately knew at that moment that I was going to climb that mountain, and that I wasn't going to be explaining to my children that I might climb it 'someday.' I was going to be telling them about the time I actually did climb the tallest mountain in the United States.

Some years later, my buddies and I were trying to figure out what we were going to do with our lives. More importantly, what were we going to do that summer. We were all making a few bucks in our menial jobs, but wanted some adventure as well. We were hanging out at my buddy Russ' house one Saturday evening like we always did, drinking beer and watching Saturday Night Live, when we started talking about going camping. Mount Whitney was still burned on my brain and I suggested that we camp up at Whitney Portal. They asked what and where it was. After I explained to them the story of Mount Whitney, our camping idea turned into excitement as we started planning out the revamped mountain climbing trip. Before I knew it, my friends Russ, Steve, and Russ' younger brother John and I were all in my 1977 Buick driving to Mount Whitney in the middle of the night. The date was August 8, 1981; we were young, we were determined, and we were all pumped with excitement.

Russ was one of my best friends all through high school. He was a tall, lanky individual who could always make you laugh just by looking at him because you just knew he was going to say or do something funny at any moment. His brother John was a character that always seemed to be getting into some kind of trouble. I could really tell that he looked up to his big brother and seemed to hang out with us quite frequently. Steve was my girlfriend Karen's brother and was always a very fun person to be with. Steve, Karen and I all worked together at my mom's restaurant, and that is where we all met. Then there was me: I was having the time of my life. I had just graduated high school, I had a crappy job making minimum wage as a parking lot attendant at a local race track, I had an awesome girlfriend, and I now had a bunch of crazy people piled into my car headed off into the great unknown. We had no idea what we were doing or getting ourselves into. We didn't plan anything at all. We just grabbed what we thought we would need and we hit the road.

We arrived at the Whitney Portal very early the next morning feeling woozy from all of the Doritos, Frito-Lay bean dip, and Dr. Pepper we consumed during the trip up there. Our ears were also still ringing from the loud punk rock music we had been listening to for those past three hours on the road. We found a parking spot and located a place near the beginning of the trail to get a few hours of shuteye, not knowing that we should had made reservations to be able to sleep in the camp. There were no available campsites, so in total darkness we found a spot behind some trees and made the best of it waking up half of the camp in the process; I will never forget the looks and sarcastic comments we got from our neighboring campers that following morning. We got an early jump that morning and started on what would one day become one of the major goals of my life: To stand on the highest point of every state in the United States. Of course at that time I wasn't even thinking about something as nutty as that; that came a little later.

We should not have even been on this mountain. Doing a climb like this takes a lot of preparation; including making sure you have both the health and stamina to accomplish such a monumental task. You need to acclimate and hydrate your body. You need to pack the correct food and gear to what type of mountain you are going to climb. You need to take care of permits, reservations… we had none of this. We were just a small group of wide-eyed teens with one goal in mind: to get to the top.

The climb was going to take us two days. The first day would get us to a place called Trail Camp that would serve as our base, and the second day would get us to the top, then all the way back down the mountain to my car. About half way to Trail Camp, we were stopped by a Park Ranger asking to see our

permits. Permits? I had no idea permits were required. Really? I
didn't know what to say or do as the Ranger stood there looking
us all over from head to toe with a condescending smirk on his
weathered face. I knew he was thinking to himself how
inexperienced we were, and I knew that he knew we didn't have
any permits. I think Russ saw the look of concern on my face
and immediately jumped in to save the day. "Our Aunt Margaret
has the permits."

We all looked at the Ranger who was now looking at Russ
with a very skeptical eye. "Your Aunt Margaret? Uh huh. And
where's she at?" We all looked at Russ for the answer when
John said, "She's behind us down the trail somewhere. We
haven't seen her for a couple hours."

"And what does your Aunt Margaret look like?"

Steve then went on to describe our fake aunt as a rickety old
lady who, after hearing his description, had no business being
with us on a climb like this in the first place. We were in real
trouble now. How were we ever going to get out of this one? I
knew the Ranger knew he had us, but unbelievably he let us
proceed with our hike. He jotted our names into his little
notebook, and let us off with a stern warning that he would
come looking for us if he couldn't find our aunt. Of course we
knew he would never find her, and we ended up constantly
looking over our shoulders for the next couple of days. Boy that
was a narrow escape.

Because we had no idea what Mount Whitney looked like,
every time we thought we saw the mountain, we would stop and
take a picture of us pointing at it. After several disappointments,
we finally gave up on this stupid idea to save on film. Back in
those days, cameras used film, and we were very limited as to
how many photographs we could take. Also all day during the
hike, Russ and John kept themselves pumped by singing the
same Black Flag song over and over and over… "We've got
nothing better to do, than watch T.V. and have a couple of

brews!" Whenever the four of us got separated throughout the day, we always knew exactly where Russ and John were.

Steve was vastly out of shape and was having a hard time keeping up with the group as the day wore on. I knew we didn't have much further to Trail Camp, so I stayed back with him to make sure that he made it in safely. He was my very good friend, and I didn't want to leave him behind. I also did not want to have to go looking for him later that night if he didn't make it. That would have been bad, especially being in very unfamiliar territory at high altitudes. I told the others to continue on and that we would arrive some time shortly behind them. All I could hear as they made their way up the mountain was, "We've got nothing better to do, than watch T.V. and have a couple of brews!" As it turned out, we were only about thirty minutes from Trail Camp and we were all back together again in no time.

Again with no permits or reservations, we were faced with having to find a suitable place to camp for the night. Trail Camp is well above the timber line, so no trees or shade this time, just a lot of rocks and the open sky. Russ had found us a nice little clearing big enough for the four of us to lay out our sleeping bags. We all claimed our spots and started thinking about our evening feast. I was feeling absolutely famished as I pulled my dinner from my backpack: a delicious freeze dried macaroni and cheese dinner conveniently packaged in a space-age foil pouch.

"Hmmm. Let's see," I read aloud," to prepare, just add boiling water and let stand for five minutes. Hey Russ, hand over the matches."

"Matches?" Russ replied with a worried look on his face, "I thought you had the matches. John, (directed to his brother) do you have any matches?"

"No. Do you have the matches Steve?"

"Nope."

"Russ! You said you were gonna bring the matches! Now what are we going to do?"

"Well John, I think you are the only person who needs them, so the question is: what are *you* going to do?"

I started looking around and noticed that there was no wood anywhere to even start a fire. Being as far above the timber line as we were would cause a problem like this. God we were so unprepared.

"You know what I'm gonna do Russ? I am going to enjoy my dinner, matches or not"

I had never had ice cold, crunchy, freeze dried macaroni and cheese before. Damn it was awful. The cheese wouldn't dissolve, the pasta stuck to my teeth, and it was literally ice-cold as I had used water from snow-melt. It was so bad. I sat there and watched the others enjoying their sandwiches, canned stew, granola bars, etc., and knew I had to choke this stuff down to get some nourishment in me. Russ, laughing to himself about my dinner situation, went down to the creek to wash his dishes. While he was gone, John offered to sell me a can of Dinty Moore Beef Stew for .50 cents. Was he kidding me? I swiftly gave him the money, opened it, and drank it right out of the can. It really hit the spot, and I was at that moment truly a happy camper. Just about the time as I was finishing licking the inside of the can perfectly clean like a starving puppy, Russ came walking up and noticed that I was eating *HIS* food!

"Where did you get that, John?" he asked quite angrily.

"I bought it from John," I replied.

Russ snatched the can out of my hands and proceeded to hit John repeatedly in the head with it. It was starting to turn into a good fight when they both collapsed to the ground due to the high elevation and lack of oxygen. As it turned out, John had sold me Russ' only other can of food, but John didn't care. He just continued to laugh while enduring Russ' beating. What made the whole thing even funnier was when they started to fight over who owned the .50 cents. They argued about this for about an hour until John finally gave up and handed over the riches to Russ.

The next day we awoke early and prepared for the final ascent. Because Steve had such a hard time getting to where we were the day before, he revealed to us that he would not be joining us on the climb to the top. We all tried in vain to get him to come with us, but he just was not interested. As the three of us left camp, I looked back and saw Steve crawl back into the warmth of his sleeping bag. I thought about what we were going to accomplish later that morning and what he was going to miss. He was so close and who knew if he would ever have such an opportunity again.

From Trail Camp to the summit was only four miles, but it was also 2,500 feet of elevation gain and we were already in thin air. It was tough. I remember my dad telling me that when you are that high, you can only walk about one hundred feet before you have to stop and rest to catch your breath, and he was right. I was doing this a lot when I got over 13,000 feet, but finally hit my stride and was able to go about five hundred feet at a time before I had to stop for a short micro break. It was even tough to walk when the trail was flat. As I neared the summit I thought about Steve back at camp and was glad that he had made the decision to stay back. I really did not think that he would have made the last couple miles.

There was a point on the trail where I could see the summit about one half mile out in the distance. What a feeling that was. I was only minutes away from standing atop the highest mountain in the country. Even though it was so close, it was also still so far. Walking a half mile in the city would take the average person about ten minutes to accomplish. I was still about 45 minutes away due to the elevation and terrain. I found myself back in the one hundred feet and rest pattern, but every time I stopped my excitement grew as I saw I was getting closer and closer to the summit. I can still remember when I took my last rest before reaching the top. I was only about two hundred feet away and could now see and hear all of the other people that had made it there before us that morning. I could hear all of the congratulations, the laughing, and the stories. I had to get there in a hurry so I could be a part of this.

My excitement pushed me the final distance and I made it to the summit to cheering, congratulations, and pats on the back from total strangers. What a sense of accomplishment that was. It was tough, but I did it. I was so proud of myself. The only other time in my life when I was this proud was when I graduated high school just a couple months prior. That was huge, and this was a very close second. I also couldn't wait to get back home to tell my dad; after all it was because of him that I was standing there on top of America in the first place. Russ and John also arrived on the summit just minutes behind me, and they too were just as exhilarated as I was. What a great moment that was for the three of us.

There is never really much more to say after a triumph like this. As with any major accomplishment, it is always what leads up to and includes the exciting finale that makes it what it is; not the after. I took some photos, congratulated others as they too made it to the top, signed the register, and then headed back down to camp. A register is usually located on every highpoint so people can record that they were there. I enjoyed reading other people's entries; one in particular said, "Where is the McDonald's?" That sounded to me like something my dad would have written.

When we got back down to Trail Camp, we found Steve still sleeping in his bag. We woke his butt up to share what he had missed. He was happy we all made it and then told us that 'our' ranger had come snooping around through the area. Steve said that he didn't want any confrontation, so he stayed hidden in his bag until the ranger left. We didn't care anymore about the ranger. What could he do to us at this point? Kick us off the mountain? We quickly packed everything up and completed our eight mile trek back to the car by nightfall. I remember somewhere on the way down, I slipped on a loose section of trail and ended up flat on my back looking straight up at Russ and John. Without any hesitation, Russ transformed himself into a major league baseball umpire, squatted, spread out his arms, and shouted "Safe!"

"Will you help me up you ass!?"

As soon as we were all in the car and heading home, our carload of teenaged over achievers were all starving for some real food; especially me. We stopped in Lone Pine for a good meal, and the only thing I remember from that was downing two large glasses of ice-cold, whole milk one after the other. God that was good.

When I walked through the front door of my house late that night, my dad immediately greeted me and wanted to know all of the details of the climb. I told him everything right down to the McDonald's entry in the register. He really got a kick out of my story and again made a comment that he would like to climb it someday. I told him that if he really ever wanted to do it, that I would do it with him. It was late and I was exhausted, so I excused myself to get cleaned up and get into bed.

I was still reeling in my success that night lying in bed. I started to wonder about the other 49 states, and if they had a highest mountain as well. Of course they did. Why wouldn't they? Did people in those states climb their highest mountains like what I had just done? Did anybody even climb those mountains at all for that matter? The following day, I went to a Thrifty Drug Store and bought a Rand McNally road atlas. I took it home and stayed up all night locating the highpoints for every state in the Nation. After I located them all, I wrote down their names, locations and elevations on the back of some crumpled Spanish homework I found tucked away in my desk drawer. I sat there and studied the list for quite a while, then all of a sudden got a rush of excitement when I suggested to myself that I should someday climb them all. Was this possible? I was just 17, right out of high school, and America was so big. How could somebody like me accomplish something so extreme and so grand? But I knew that I really wanted to do this.

As I studied the map, states like Montana, Vermont, and North Carolina all seemed so far away. That was because they *were* so far away. There was no way I could ever travel that far. How could I? And I sure didn't want to do them alone. Who could I ever talk into doing something like this with me? I talked to Russ about it one day and he said, "Sure John! No problem! Let's do it!" But that was Russ. I knew that he would never really do it. He could never really commit to anything back then, and never had any money just like the rest of us.

After my excitement died down a few days later, I came to the realization that it was just too impossible of an idea. I stuffed the paper back into my desk drawer and never looked at it again. Honestly, I don't even remember what happened to it. I probably threw it away on one of those rare occasions when I actually took time to clean my room properly. I also never hiked with Russ, John, or Steve again either. Life happened and we all went our own separate ways after that amazing summer of 1981.

Russ had always been a character ever since the first day I met him. I still vividly remember the day we met in high school. We were all standing under a tree on campus and I was holding onto a branch above my head as we talked. Russ looked over at me and said with a straight face, "Why are you shaking that tree branch John? There's no oranges up there." As odd as this sounds, we all broke into hysterical laughter. His kind of humor was so very different, and that is what drew everybody to him. He just had that personality that everybody loved. Later in life, he enlisted in the Air Force where he specialized in Fire

Protection. He ended up as a fireman in the Los Angeles County Fire Department when he got out, and I have always been extremely proud of him for that accomplishment.

His brother John and I never really hung out that much, as he was a little younger and we really didn't have anything in common. He passed away during the writing of this memoir and never knew I was writing it or even that he was mentioned in it for that matter. It was a sad occasion, especially since he was only 44 years old and died of heart failure. I attended his memorial service where we were asked to share our personal stories of John. I did not hesitate for a moment to share my Dinty Moore Beef Stew story with all of his friends and family. It got a good laugh and I heard somebody say, "Yep! That was John!" Even though I had been out of touch with him for so many years, he will be greatly missed and I do think about him from time to time.

Steve and I stayed very good friends, even after his sister Karen and I had broken up. Sometime in 1982, he was in a horrific automobile accident. He had suffered serious head trauma and was hospitalized for months near my place of employment. I would go and visit him every chance I had; which was almost daily. It was during my last visit that I sadly and unexpectedly lost him as a friend forever.

He had been expecting me when I walked into his room and found him sitting there on the edge of his bed. He had only been strong enough to do this for the previous week or so, and I remember what a triumph it was when he had done it for the first time. He could barely hold his head up due to the injury, so I would always grab a chair and sit near him so we could make eye contact and visit. It was during this visit that he told me not to bother with the chair. He angrily told me to leave and that he never wanted to see me again. I was shocked and asked why. He wouldn't tell me and insisted that I leave, so I finally did as he asked. I didn't really take him seriously when he said that he never wanted to see me again, but I did feel that it was a little harsh. I was really curious as to why he was so angry, or better yet, what it was he thought that I did to make him feel this way. I thought it best to leave and maybe come back in a day or two to see if things changed.

As I was walking through the hospital towards the exit, I saw Karen with another of Steve's friends, as well as with another guy who I assumed was her new boyfriend. I knew all of Steve and Karen's friends, and didn't recognize this guy. They were all walking towards me, and we hesitantly said hello as we passed. I heard one of them say something under their breath, and then all of them started laughing. I turned back to look at them, and found that they were all looking back at me as well. With this, I assumed that what was said was said at my expense. I walked out the front door of the hospital very hurt and confused as to everything that had just occurred in the last few minutes. I stopped just outside the exit door and immediately decided to go back to his room to get some answers. I didn't really care about what had just occurred with my ex-girlfriend, but Steve and I were the best of friends and I deserved to know what the hell was going on.

When I got back to his room, he was still very angry and told me to leave again. I insisted that he tell me why he was doing this and he repeatedly shouted loudly, "Get out!" I finally left when one of the nurses told me to leave. I tried calling him later that evening as well as many times more over the next several days. He refused all of my calls until one day I was told that he had been discharged the previous evening. I called his mom's house where he lived, and the number had been changed. This was all so confusing and hurtful to an 18 year old. I talked to some people about what happened and learned that many head trauma patients go through this sort of anger phase. I always thought that every phase had a beginning and an end, but this particular one never came to any type of conclusion. Even as I write this over thirty years later I still feel some heartache and confusion. I will never fully understand what or why it happened. I just hope that his life got back on track and today he is happy. He certainly deserves it.

As for me, I worked the rest of 1981 at my mom's restaurant. It was in November of that year that I interviewed for a job at Hughes Aircraft Company, and accepted a position as an electrical technician that following month. I was the first one of us that actually had a 40 hour per week job, which helped escalate the process of us all drifting apart. We were all basically becoming adults with jobs and girlfriends. None of us had the time to hang out as much as we used to anymore. It is sad how we allow these things to happen.

Fast-forward to sometime in 1991 when I was talking to a buddy of mine at work by the name of Mike about my long, lost, crazy dream of summiting all the highpoints in the United States. He was an avid hiker, and I told him about my Mount Whitney climb, my Rand McNally purchase, my list of the state highpoints, and finally my dream to climb them all. To my amazement, he said, "That's awesome! Let's do it! I'll do them with you if you still want to do it!" And he meant it. I couldn't believe that somebody else would want to do something as nutty as this. It was just a ridiculous dream to me; a huge dream that just seemed too impossible. But then, we're talking about Mike here. He was a crazy guy himself who liked doing crazy stuff. We went into my office so I could show him what I was talking about, and we ended up planning out our first few highpoints right there on the spot: Arizona, California (again?), and Nevada.

Chapter 3
- The Mad Dash!

I had made a decision a number of years earlier that if I ever had the opportunity to chase my highpointing dream that I would only do the lower 48 states and not all 50 as I had originally planned. This was due to Denali in Alaska. Too many people had died on that mountain over the years; very experienced people. I had too much to live for, and just did not want to take that kind of risk. And because I was not going to do Alaska, I didn't need to do Hawaii. It was either the Lower 48 states, or all 50. Mike planned on doing all 50 states, and to that I gave him by blessings. It was also because of this mindset that I would end up making a few extreme decisions during my highpointing journey all the way up to its unfortunate conclusion many years later.

Mike had somehow stumbled upon a book entitled "Highpoints of the United States" by Don W. Holmes, which was a guide to the fifty state summits. We each obtained a copy and had it autographed by Don, who was himself a fifty peak completer. I also joined a club for highpointers conveniently called "The Highpointers Club." I was around the 500th person to join, and at the time of this writing, its membership had swelled to well into the thousands. I made it my goal to be a 48 peak completer, and I wanted to be one of the first one hundred people ever to accomplish it. When I joined, the total number was about 85. I felt I had a fair enough chance of meeting this goal and I wanted to get started right away. It took Mike and I about a month to plan our first climb in Arizona, and before I knew it, I was well on my way to realizing the beginning stages of my highpointing dreams were finally coming true.

Arizona Humphreys Peak
12,633' June 23, 1991

I belonged to a hiking club within our company called the HAC Packers (HAC stood for Hughes Aircraft Company). I put out a notice in our monthly club newsletter asking if anyone wanted to join Mike and me on our upcoming Arizona adventure. Another club member by the name of John replied to the invitation and promptly joined in on our escapade. Mike was vacationing in Las Vegas the weekend of the climb, so John and I drove up there to pick him up at his hotel. We found him in the hotel's casino playing quarter craps. All we had to do when we walked into the casino was to listen for the, "Yo 'leven!" and there he was. Before we left the hotel, Mike went to his room and made himself a free pot of coffee; an activity that would be played out over and over again during our future years-long journey. Once he was fully caffeinated, we piled into his Isuzu and headed off to the highlands of Arizona. On the way, we stopped somewhere in Nevada for what would become the beginning of one of our first highpointing traditions: Subway sandwiches. We didn't know it at the time, but something about their food always kept us coming back for more during our highpointing adventures.

During Mike's life, he was affectionately known as Mr. Cheap. Nobody would ever argue with me on this point, not even Mike. He reused everything to its limits, and spent as minimal as possible. When he is waiting for the water to get hot in his shower, he catches the cold water in buckets to use in his garden. Instead of throwing a piece of paper away, he will cut it into smaller pieces and use the backsides as notepads. When he accelerates from a traffic signal or a stop sign, he will let the car get up to speed on its own terms in order to save gas. There are many, many examples like this, but here is the best one of all: Mike lives in a very affluent neighborhood where all of his neighbor's houses are just simply beautiful: Manicured yards, nice cars in the driveways, you get the idea. His house looks like it belongs on skid row, and he is extremely proud of that fact. A beautifully remodeled home across the street from him sat on the market for months, and never sold. After the sign came down, Mike went over and knocked on the owner's door to tell them why nobody wanted to purchase their house. The owner of course was very interested as Mike began to explain. He actually told him that the prospective buyers most-likely loved the house, but when they walked out the front door and saw what was sitting directly across the street, they said, "No way!" Mike further explained to the owner that if *he* replaced the stucco and repainted his house, he would have a better chance of selling his own. Some colorful words were exchanged between them, and over twenty years later, Mike's house still looks the same as it ever did. To this day, Mike proudly says that his middle initial (Michael C. Gauthier) stands for 'cheap'.

Mike drove his little car 55 miles per hour the entire way to Flagstaff. What a looooooong drive that was. I believe it took us six hours when it should have taken about four. He wouldn't let John or I share in the driving because he was afraid that we might have reached ludicrous speeds like 56 or even 57 miles per hour which would have been a 'Huge waste of fuel'. When we finally arrived at the trailhead, we set up camp and spent that night on cots in the parking lot under the stars. It always amazes me as to how many stars you can see when you are high up in the mountains. It is simply unbelievable and so beautiful.

The next morning I was the first to awake and was extremely eager to get started. This was eleven years in the making since the day I created that list from my road atlas, and it was finally becoming a reality. As I began to prepare for my very first highpoint, I was disappointed to learn that I had forgotten my brand new hiking boots I had just purchased for the occasion. This meant that I now had to do the entire hike in my old, worn out sneakers. I had put a lot of thought and research into purchasing those boots, and now it was all for not. This was a huge mistake on my part and I hoped that nothing would come of it. Regardless, I was anxious to get going and the other two couldn't get ready fast enough. Boots or sneakers, nothing was going to keep me from reaching my very first highpoint.

Once we got started, the beginning of the hike took us across some winter ski slopes on the west side of the mountain, then into the thick, dark woods. Once in the forest, the trail gradually steepened to a point where I had no traction because of my shoes. I managed to make it past this area, but it wasn't without a little adventure. There were a few instances where I would take a step and then feel myself begin to slide. I had to crouch over and touch my fingers to the ground as I proceeded to slip back down the trail on my finger-tips and toes. Once we broke out of the woods and were above the timberline, we found ourselves standing on the ridge of the mountain and could see the peak about a mile away.

As we eventually approached the summit, we found that quite a few people had beaten us up there that morning. It only took us about four hours to reach the top, which wasn't bad at all. I had expected it to take much longer. Overall the peak was fairly undemanding and was nothing like what I had expected, but I truly didn't know what to expect. All I had to compare it with was Mount Whitney, and it wasn't even close to being anything like that.

So there I was, standing on the top of Arizona. I now had my first highpoint completed and was so excited and proud of myself for my huge achievement. I found a small corner of the summit to take my pack off and relax a bit. I wanted to let it all soak in. People were milling about, talking, eating, taking photos; and there I was in the middle of it all. I wanted so badly to share this moment with my wife Anna, but these were the times before cell phones, and Al Gore had not invented the Internet yet. It would have to wait until later in the day when we came across a phone booth somewhere on the way back to Vegas. I couldn't wait to tell her.

I had peak number one completed, and only 47 to go. 'Wow,' I thought to myself; '47 more to go'. I realized that this was not going to be as easy as I thought it was. This was going to take some time and some money, but I was very excited and determined at this point and I actually thought that nothing could stop me. I was going to do this. I was going to get my 48 mountains.

I started a tradition up there for myself that day: I had my photo taken of me sitting on the summit while holding my highpointers book along with a small American flag. I followed this tradition all throughout my highpointing experience using the same book and flag. We spent about an hour up there and then decided it was time to go if we wanted to make the all you can eat pancake breakfast at The Boardwalk hotel and casino for $0.99. This was another of Mike's zany, money saving ideas. Why pay a lot for food when you can get it for practically free? We got back to the car and 55'd it all the way back into Las Vegas. I actually think Mike hit sixty a couple of times, but it may have been because a tail wind caught him by surprise

while traveling on the downhill portions of
Interstate 40.

I could not wait for the next mountain and we planned the
whole thing on the drive back into Vegas. It would be a
mountain that I stood atop on three previous occasions. I didn't
have to do it again, but I needed to continue my new tradition of
getting a photo taken of me holding my book and flag on top of
the summit. It was going to be California again.

*In total, I had climbed Humphrey's Peak on two separate
occasions:*
*Climb #1 was for score and was as just told here in
Chapter 3.*
*Climb #2 was completed on 7/11/1998 in preparation for
Kings Peak, UT. I had already completed 43 highpoints by this
time and really didn't want to climb it again, but Mike kept
insisting that I should in order to keep in shape for Utah. I
really had to come up with a good reason to talk myself into
driving all the way into Arizona to climb this mountain yet*

again. I took a good look at the photos of all my previous highpoints and took notice of the one thing they all had in common: I always had a photo taken of me holding my book and flag together. My first climb of Humphreys back in 1991 was the only time I had two photos taken of me; one holding my book, and the other holding my flag. I couldn't let something like that occur, and that quickly became the justification I needed to do this mountain yet again. Funny enough, I cannot for the life of me remember much about this climb no matter how hard I think about it. About all I can remember is that it was Mike, our friend Joe and myself that did the climb. I also remember that once we got to within about fifty feet of the summit that Joe made a sprint for it so he could be the first to the top. I also remember having a Mount Whitney moment when again I slipped on a loose section of trail and ended up flat on my back looking straight up at Mike and Joe this time; again, no harm, no foul.

California Mount Whitney
14,494' July 14, 1991

Most people ask me, "California again?" I did not have to climb this mountain again, but the main reason I did it (for the fifth and final time) was to continue my brand-new tradition of obtaining a photo of me at the top of each mountain holding my book and flag. Mike and I heard through the grapevine about some friends that were going to climb Mount Whitney, so we sort of invited ourselves along for the ride. I needed the photograph and this was my opportunity. I did not realize they were going to summit the peak and be back down to the cars in the same day though. I did not have much time to prepare before I totally destroyed myself doing this. I also did not realize my camera was out of film until I got to the top. Luckily, Mike brought his little 110 camera and got a shot of me up there. I had a mild case of altitude sickness while I was at the top, and I can totally see it every time I look at the photo of me sitting there on the summit.

There is one Point I want to emphasize about a hike like this: Do not, I repeat, DO NOT do this hike as a one day, day hike. Never, ever, ever! Not unless you are physically and mentally prepared. My feet swelled up so bad afterward that I had to take two days off from work. Never again will I do something as stupid at that. When we got back down to the cars, I took my boots off and plunged my swollen, blistered feet into the bone chilling waters of Lone Pine Creek to cool them off and slow the swelling. A couple days later I thought about those poor people brushing their teeth and making coffee somewhere downstream. I wonder if they noticed any strange tastes and odors in the water.

Regardless of the punishment I had put myself through that day, I now had my second highpoint officially in the books, and would have my third in just five weeks' time. It was going to be Nevada, and looking at the maps made me realize I had never been anywhere so remote and lonely before in my life. Highpointing was definitely taking me places I had never imagined or even thought about going.

In total, I had now climbed Mount Whitney four times and one failed attempt:

Climb #1 was as told in Chapter 2.

Climb #2 was with Anna. I don't recall the date we attempted it, but it was in the 1984/1985 time frame. We didn't make it. I got severe altitude sickness at Trail Camp, and I was up and miserable all night. Altitude sickness is not a fun thing. The severe headaches and nausea were just too much to bear. About the only way to get rid of it was to put my forty pound pack back on and head back down the mountain to lower elevations. Believe me; you are not up to doing that when you're feeling that awful. I was very miserable, and decided that we should head back down the mountain as soon as there was enough light to do so. One good thing though; this time I didn't forget the permits, decent food, or the matches. We did however forget a camera, so no photos.

Climb #3 was with my two friends and co-workers Pat and Irv. We summited the mountain on September 27, 1987. Again I had the permits, but it wasn't until we were about twenty miles from my house when I realized that I had left them on my kitchen counter. They still don't let me live that one down. We made it all the way to the summit without a hitch. I lugged a bottle of fine $2.95 champagne to the top to celebrate the stupendous event. About a dozen other grubby hikers joined in on the festivities.

Enjoying a sip of fine
$2.95 champagne on the summit

Climb #4 was with my co-worker Darryl, Mike, and Anna again. Darryl, Mike and I made it to the top with no problems. Anna turned back to Trail Camp at around 13,000 feet about halfway up the 98 switchbacks. Only this time there were no switchbacks, only snow and ice. It was kind of hairy. One wrong step would have probably sent us sliding back down the mountain for a mile back into Trail Camp. Anna turned around at that point and I didn't blame her. It was snow and ice for two miles beyond that point. Talk about slow going. I summited on June 4, 1989 with no problems. On the way back down, we glissaded from 13,777 feet to 12,500 feet. Glissading is when you basically slide down a mountain, in the snow, on your butt. We slid for about one mile. It was cold and it was wet, but what a time saver, and oh was it ever fun. The only drawback to glissading in Levi's 501 jeans is the fact that they absorb a hell of A LOT of water. I had to walk eight miles back to the car in

30

wet, cold pants. Another lesson learned. Do not hike in the snow or rain in cotton pants. One word: Chaffing.

I was working for Hughes Aircraft Company at the time, and our company newsletter got a hold of our story and wanted to publish a small article on our achievement. Maybe it was because we took a copy of the newsletter to the summit with us? Maybe it was because I took a photo of us at the top of the mountain reading their newsletter? Maybe it was because when we got back to work I told the company newsletter what I had done? Regardless, they did publish an article, and the three of us became instant celebrities around work for a while after that.

Climb #5 was for score and was as just told here in Chapter 3.

Mike had summited Mount Whitney on nine separate occasions; two of them with me. In a recent email of his, he stated: "My 1st Summit of Whitney was on Christmas Day 1976. One of my (few) "Claims to Fame", that I was the ONLY Person on Top of Mt. Whitney on Christmas Day in the Year of the great Bi-centennial of the United States. I went back in July of 1977 and checked the Summit Log. And sure-enough, my Entry was the only one on 12/25/76 (Wow, this Christmas Day - 2016 - that will be 40-years ago!)."

Who's news at Hughes

SCG EMPLOYEES Mike Gauthier, left, and John White read the Hughesnews atop Mt. Whitney, highest mountain in the continental United States. The fearless duo brought along the company journal to have "something to do" after the grueling two-day hike to the 14,495-foot summit.

Three adventurous SCG employees, **Darryl Dietz, Mike Gauthier, and John White,** conquered the highest mountain in the continental United States, Mt. Whitney, located out of Lone Pine in Eastern California.

The three reached the 14,495-foot summit after two grueling days of traversing ice fields and scrambling up rock piles. It was a balmy 30 degrees at the top.

Of course, we would have printed such a story anyway. It didn't matter that the trio took along a copy of the Hughesnews to read, as John said, "Because we figured when we got to the top we wouldn't have much to do.

"We just thought that you would like to know that we like your paper so much that we take it everywhere with us."

Nevada Boundary Peak
13,143' August 25, 1991

The only way I can describe this mountain is as if God himself drove his own personal dump truck into Nevada and dumped a 13,143 foot load of pea gravel onto the western border of the state. With each step I took up that mountain, it was literally one step up, and half a step down... one step up, and half a step down... and after the first step, my boots were full of gravel and there was nothing I could do about it. It was a very tough and strenuous climb.

Mike, another hiker (and coworker) by the name of Jasper, and I drove all day through the scorching Owens Valley Summer to get to Boundary Peak located way out in the loneliest part of America in a no man's land called Eastern Nevada. Because it was so hot outside, I had the air conditioning running on full at all times. About every 45 minutes or so, the fuse on the air conditioning circuit would blow and I would have to pull over to replace it. I brought along a large cache of fuses that I kept in my ash tray because this had been a recurring problem for months; and living in Southern California you have got to have your air conditioning. After the third or fourth time replacing the fuse, Mike had had enough and told me not to start the truck until we figured out what was causing the fuses to blow. As he was looking under the hood I opened the ash try to get another fuse when I spotted a shiny penny down in the cigarette lighter hole. As it turned out, the air conditioner as well as the cigarette lighter were both on the same electrical circuit; need I say more?

We stopped along the way in the tiny hamlet of Independence, California for Subway sandwiches to take along for dinner later that night. When we eventually got to our turn-off in Nevada, we followed a dirt road for twelve miles that led us directly to the trailhead. It was a good thing I had brought my truck instead of a car as this road was a real mess. It was poorly graded, full of pot-holes, sand traps, and large rocks littered the entire length. We followed the road all the way until it dead-ended into a sea of pungent smelling sage growing along a cow pie filled creek. To avoid driving down the sandy bank into the water and getting us stuck permanently, I had to turn my full-sized Ford F350 Crew Cab around. This was no easy task as I got us pinned in there pretty well. After getting stuck a few times in the gravel at nine thousand feet, I was finally able to get it turned around and back down to a good level area where we would camp for the night.

As soon as we got settled, out came the Subway sandwiches. We were camped in an area where we couldn't see the mountain we would be conquering the next day, but we all ate our soggy sandwiches facing the general direction of the mountain sharing stories of our previous hikes and climbs. After dinner, Jasper packed up his gear and started off into the mountains. We asked where he was going and he told us that he liked to be alone with nature in places like this, so he was going to go as far as he could before it got too dark. We wished him luck and told him we would be looking for him in the morning.

Mike and I planned to sleep in the bed of my truck that night and start our hike around 6:00AM the next morning. He went inside the truck to read a book while I lay on top of my bedding staring up at the heavens. There was a constant strong wind blowing that night and I literally watched thousands of flies and bugs shooting through the evening sky over my truck like tiny black meteorites all going in the same direction as if they were all attending a bug convention somewhere up the mountain. Every once in a while, I heard one hit the side of my truck so hard, they sounded like small rocks, 'Ping!'

Darkness settled quickly and it started getting pretty cold as I crawled into the warmth of my flannel lined sleeping bag. The full moon rose above the ridge of the mountain and was so brilliant that it was as if it was daytime instead of night. It was way too bright to get any decent sleep, not to mention the cold wind that was blowing. I had to keep my head buried in my sleeping bag as best as possible to make it as dark and as warm as I could to get some good sleep before the next day's grueling climb. Mike ended up sleeping in the back seat of my truck to stay warm while I toughed it out in the elements.

The next morning, we headed up the mountain following faint cow trails, sidestepping cow pies and dodging thick pockets of flies. We kept working our way up the mountain and eventually came upon where Jasper had spent the previous night; which was about two miles up from our camp. He had spent the night at a place called Trail Canyon Saddle, and had left his backpack there. We figured he had about a two hour head start on us. We proceeded up the 'gravel' mountain to look for the summit as well as for Jasper. It was very tough climbing those last two thousand feet in elevation of loose gravel. I tried to outsmart the mountain by boulder hopping, but every time I got on a rock big enough for me to stand on, it would begin to slide. It's a strange feeling when you jump on a rock the size of a Buick and it starts to move downhill with you perched on it like a frightened cat. I eventually came to realize that the easiest way to continue the climb was to just walk through the gravel, so that's the approach I took for the rest of the climb.

After a couple exhausting hours, we finally made it to the top where Jasper was still nowhere to be found. We located the register which was in an old ARMY ammo container, and noticed that Jasper had been there some two hours prior just as we figured. Since Boundary Peak was only a quarter mile from the California border, and about a half mile from the nearest 13,000 foot peak in California (Montgomery Peak), we figured that Jasper had decided to head on over to bag that one as well; which he did. What an animal that man was.

On top of Nevada with
Montgomery Peak, CA in the background

It was when I started enjoying my delicious lunch of tuna salad and crackers when it finally hit me that I was sitting on top of my third highpoint. I put my food down, stood up, and did a complete, slow 360 degree panoramic view of the countryside. Mike asked what I was doing and I replied, "Just letting it all soak in my friend... just letting it all soak in." After shooing a few birds away from attempting to steal my lunch, I sat back down and enjoyed the rest of my meal. Afterward, as I was signing the register, I started up a conversation with Mike on what would be our fourth highpoint. We both threw around a few ideas, but nothing really stuck. The only thing we were able to agree on was that there would be a fourth highpoint, and a fifth highpoint, and so on. At this point, I had three highpoints down, and 45 left to go. I still had such a very long journey ahead of me.

Being so remote, we only saw two other people up there, and it was only as we were leaving the peak. On our hike back down to the truck, we took a short-cut off the mountain which turned out to be about a two thousand foot elevation drop within a one mile span. It was great. We ran down through the gravel, sometimes leaping ten to fifteen feet at a time. When we got down to where it leveled out, we dumped all the gravel out of our boots where we formed Nevada's next highest high points. We worked our way back down the valley along the smelly, flying insect infested creek to the comfort of my waiting truck.

On the drive back home, we stopped back into the same Subway we had just visited the day before. During my highpointing days, I tried to keep myself in shape by eating right. Because of this, every time I went into a Subway, I always got their Veggie Delight which had no meat, only veggies. And because you can build your sandwich at Subway anyway you wish, I always had that sandwich bursting at the seams with every veggie they had to offer (with the exception of onions and bell peppers... yuk).

A little over five months after completing this mountain, Anna and I welcomed our first child into our lives; our amazing son Zachary. Sometime after that I had decided it was time to capture a few more summits. I wanted to do a few that were further away from home this time and called Mike to see if he was interested. His life was a little busy at the time and he didn't have much occasion to travel. He did however squeeze in a trip to Hawaii about a month after Boundary Peak where he was able to summit Hawaii's highpoint Mauna Kea. He invited me to come along for the ride, but because of my previous decision in only doing the lower 48 states, I could not justify the trip. Even though I wanted to get a few more highpoints, I really had no idea which ones to shoot for. That all changed when my dad invited us all to come visit him in Atlanta, Georgia. Before we went, I called my dad and talked him into taking me to a few of the local highpoints. I figured we could get Georgia, Tennessee, North Carolina, and South Carolina's highpoints all within one day. Boy was I wrong.

In total, I had climbed Boundary Peak twice:
Climb #1 was for score and was as told here in Chapter 3.
Climb #2 was in preparation for my Borah Peak climb, and is as told in Chapter 15.

Chapter 4
- All That Way for This!?

I awoke early to find dad alone in his dining room drinking a cup of coffee and studying some road maps of where we were heading out to that day. The sun was just beginning to peer through the curtains which meant that everybody else would soon be up as well. As I was pouring myself a cup in the kitchen, he asked me, "Are you sure about all of this?" I obviously answered "Yes" as I walked back into the dining room and sat down beside him to look over the maps. After some talking and renegotiating we ended up trimming the road trip down from four peaks to two with a deal that we would do a third if time permitted; the two would be Georgia and Tennessee. As they say, 'I guess my eyes were a little bigger than my stomach.' We all piled into my dad's '77 Lincoln, had a quick breakfast at the local Waffle House, then headed North into Georgia's high country.

Georgia Brasstown Bald
4,784' September 10, 1992

The excitement in me was building the closer we got to the mountain, and I just couldn't wait to get there. I felt like a child going to Disneyland, and we just couldn't get there fast enough. The drive was a little longer than what I had anticipated due to several pit stops for the ladies so they could do some sight-seeing and shopping along the way. I figured I owed them that for spending a whole day cooped up in a car with me chasing my batty ambitions.

As we neared the mountain, we easily found the parking lot and the foot path that would take us to the top of Georgia. The pathway was a little steep, but was paved and only a half mile in distance to the top. This was much different than I had become accustomed too; hiking miles on rocky, dirt trails at high elevations. When we got to the summit, my dad stopped, looked around, and said in disbelief, "You have *got* to be kidding me. We came all that way for this?!"

I looked at him, smiled, and replied, "Yep!"

"This isn't even a mountain. It's more like a molehill."

"Yep, but mountain or molehill, I need to do them all."

"How many of the other state highpoints are like this one?"

"I don't know, probably about half of them."

"Is Tennessee going to be like this one?"

"Probably."

"You gotta be a little nuts to be doing something like this."

"Maybe a little."

I know my dad didn't really think I was nuts, and it really wouldn't have mattered much anyway if he did. I was just so thrilled and happy to be standing on my fourth highpoint, and even more so that it was all of the way across the country this time. This was the first highpoint for my dad, Anna, Zachary, and for my step-mom Carol. I proudly told them that they all now qualified as highpointers which was then met with a collective yawn. I hurried them to take some photos and get back to the car so we could start making our way up into Tennessee. We had some time to make up and I didn't want to waste any more of it than what was necessary. The way I saw it, there was still a chance of getting a third highpoint that day.

As soon as we got in the car, Anna suggested that she had had enough and thought we should maybe start heading back down to my dad's house. It had already been a long day and we had Zachary to think of as well. I told her that the next highpoint in Tennessee was only a few short hours away, and if I didn't get it now I would probably never get it. I also expressed to her and my family how important all of this was to me, and that we couldn't turn back now since we were so close. They all happily agreed and we continued on our journey north. They all still thought I was a little nutty for doing something like this, but they really did enjoy themselves and looked forward to visiting the next peak. As for me, I was so ecstatic that I had another highpoint under my belt, and even more so that I was going to have a couple more before the day was out.

Tennessee Clingmans Dome
6,643' September 10, 1992

As we were parking the car at the trailhead to Clingmans Dome, my dad said, "This better be a lot more exciting than the last one, boy."

My immediate response was, "This is going to be *just* as exciting as the last one for me!"

This mountain was another easy one. Like Brasstown Bald, the trail was also paved all the way to the top and was only one half mile long. My dad and Carol accompanied me to the summit while Anna stayed back in the car with Zachary. He was sleeping and it was raining (my first of many peaks in the rain).

The trail and the peak were completely covered in spruce-fir, and a very cleverly designed observation tower on the top allowed for a 360 degree uninterrupted view of the Great Smokey Mountains. When I walked up the spiraling ramp to the top of the overlook, it took me up through the trees to a point where it was like I was actually walking on the tops of them. It was very cool to say the least. It didn't really matter that I climbed the tower though since I couldn't even see two feet out in front of me due to the thick fog. My dad looked out from the tower and said, "I guess this is why they call these the Great Smokey Mountains."

There was a steady, hard drizzle and it was getting rather cold up there. We didn't bring any protective gear, so I had my dad quickly take my photo and then we all went back down to the car in a hurry. When I got back, I opened the door where Anna was sitting and told her to go up while I stayed back in the car with Zack. She said that she didn't feel like going. I asked why and she said, "I don't know. I just don't feel like it."

"Are you sure?" I asked.

"Yes. Now come on and get in the car. You're letting all the cold air in."

"Are you sure?"

"Yes I am sure. Going up there isn't really that important to me, and it's cold, and it's raining…"

"Come on. I'll go with you. Zack can stay here in the car with dad & Carol."

She still didn't want to go. I then gave her one last plea, "You have to go. You're so close. We traveled 2,500 miles to get to this point, and now you only have one easy half mile to go. Come on. I'll go with you."

She looked at me and said, "Johnny, this is important to you, not to me. I am very glad you got this mountain, but I don't

44

need or want too because I don't plan on doing many of the other highpoints with you either. Now please get in the car."

I closed her door, and thought about what she said as I walked around to the other side. I totally understood where she was coming from. I had already completed five mountains to this point, and she only had Georgia as well as her two unsuccessful attempts on Mount Whitney. I had hoped that she got the same feeling I did when standing on the tops of these peaks, but since her only peak was back in Georgia, and it was nothing short of being absolutely dull, I fully understood her feelings. I got into the car, leaned over and gave her a kiss and a smile. I did want her to be a part of my highpointing experiences, but in the end it was all OK. We would have many other experiences we could share; just not any where highpointing was involved.

It was getting rather dark and late, so we called off the third peak which would have been Sassafras Mountain in South Carolina. It was only an extra hour out of the way headed back to my dad's place, but we were all getting a little tired and stir crazy in the car. It was definitely time to start heading back. There would be another day, another opportunity, and that mountain wasn't going anywhere. Climbing Sassafras would end up being only a few short years away, but unfortunately the circumstances around that climb wouldn't be as joyful.

On the drive back to my dad's house we stopped off in the small town of Cherokee, North Carolina to get something to eat. Just as we were finishing our meal, a man came rushing into the restaurant yelling for everybody to get their belongings and get out quickly because there was a flash flood coming down out of the Mountains. Just like everybody else in the restaurant, we left in one hell of a hurry. I couldn't believe how quickly that placed cleared out. When we eventually got back to my dad's house several hours later and turned on the news, we saw that a flash flood had in fact come through Cherokee and really messed things up. There was some footage showing a mobile home stuck up in some trees. It had also caused some serious damage to bridges, homes, and campgrounds, and property damage was estimated in the millions of dollars. Luckily there were no deaths or injuries. Witnesses reported seeing a wall of water roaring down the stream and had only minutes to run for safety. We surmised that we were some of those people. Thank goodness we were warned to leave. We were so very lucky.

What a long day that turned out to be. I know I could have attained all four peaks if I were alone or with another fellow highpointer. It is hard to do things like this with a family in tow because you need to deal with other issues not pertaining to mountains that end up eating a lot of time. Being alone or with a fellow climber, you have one goal in mind and nothing gets in your way. I do however look back on those two mountains as a highlight to my story. It was nice to share them with my family, and for them to see and understand what it was that I was trying to accomplish.

Up to this point, my dad and Anna had some reservations about my dream of traveling all over the country and climbing these mountains. I know they had their doubts that I could actually pull it off, but now that I had several peaks under my belt, and they had witnessed how rewarding this whole thing was for me, they finally accepted the fact that I was on a mission and that it was all very possible.

Chapter 5
- Rocky Mountain Express

Several months had passed since my trip to see dad, and I was itching to get another highpoint completed. Because the highpoints were getting further away from California, driving to them by car wasn't really as feasible for me anymore; at least not during that time frame of my highpointing quest. It was for this reason that my highpointing was slowing down to a crawl. At the rate I was going, I wouldn't be completing all 48 mountains until I was well into my seventies. This just was not acceptable to me, and I needed to get this process sped up somehow. I eventually got a climb planned, and it would be almost exactly a year before I was triumphantly standing on top of one high up in the Rocky Mountains.

Colorado Mount Elbert
14,433' September 4, 1993

This mountain was a great one for me. After it was successfully completed, my attitude towards the whole highpointing thing grew even stronger. Not only do I think it was because I knocked out the second highest highpoint in the country, but also because I found somebody as crazy as I was who didn't care about flying off to far away cities, renting cars, driving all night, hiking all day, eating cheap food, sleeping in airports and in cars... who else do you know that would do something like that besides my good friend Mike?

My dad worked for Delta airlines at the time, and I was able to fly for practically free to anywhere in the 48 states, so Mike and I both traveled to Denver on separate airlines at separate times. Why didn't Mike fly with me on Delta? Because he found an airline that would get him to Denver for about $17.38 less than what I paid. Remember? Cheap. I arrived in Denver at 10:00AM, while Mike's flight wasn't due there until 8:00 that evening. I had a lot of time to kill, so I rented a car, drove around Denver, toured the foothills a little, took in a movie at a local theater (I saw Sliver with Sharon Stone and it was absolutely awful), got something to eat, then went back to the airport to pick up Mike.

As we started into the Rockies, Mike required his coffee fix so we pulled into some tiny little town off of Interstate 70 and found a place that was just closing up for the night. When we asked if we could get some coffee, the store keeper didn't hesitate to reopen the shop and brew us a fresh pot. He filled both of our Thermoses and only charged us for one. There sure are a lot of great people in this world.

During the drive to the mountain that night, Mike and I talked a lot about hiking in the high country. I had mentioned to him that I regularly suffered from altitude sickness when I got too high up; sometimes mild, and sometimes very acute. He taught me a few basics about climbing successfully into high elevations:

- Drink so much fluid the day and night before the hike that you have to urinate about every twenty minutes, and urinate clear.
- Sleep as high up on the mountain as you can the night before the hike to get better acclimated to the higher elevations.
- Drink plenty of fluids during the hike as well, so much so that again you will have to urinate often and clear.

Because hiking mountains of this magnitude is very strenuous on the body, and I did not want to suffer through another bout of altitude sickness, I thought I would give his three steps to mountain climbing success a try. I immediately started drinking even more water than I already was the rest of the way to the mountain, and I did have to make a couple extra pit stops in the process. Once there, we found a good spot to park for the night, we downed a lot of water, and then tried to get some sleep. It didn't take me very long to realize that I was not keeping up with Mike's teachings as he woke up about every thirty minutes to relieve himself all through the night and I did not have to do this once. We slept in the rental car and the dome light turning on and off all night drove me nuts. It was so cold outside that by the time the car warmed back up from his previous urinary expedition, he would have to go back outside again for another round. And to top it all off, he would take a few more huge gulps of water before he went back to sleep! He told me on a couple occasions, "You're not drinking enough."

I told him, "You're not sleeping enough."

There is only so much water a person can drink. I only hoped that I had consumed enough to get me through the following day.

We were camped in a deep canyon at ten thousand feet in elevation with Mount Elbert to the south of us, and Mount Massive, which is the third highest mountain in the 48 states, to the north. Mount Elbert is only 65 feet shorter than Mount Whitney, and Mount Massive is only twelve feet shorter than Mount Elbert. All during the climb, Mike would point over to Mount Massive and say something like, "Look at that giant mountain over there. It sure is huge" or, "It sure is enormous" I swear he ended up using every possible word in the thesaurus other than the word 'massive' that day to describe that mountain. At one point he asked if we should stay an extra day to climb Mount Massive. My response was, "I don't know if I will be up to climbing something so giant and colossal. It's just so immense!"

As for Mike's high country mountain climbing tips, I was skeptical that any of it would work at first, but I totally swear by it now. I am usually pretty trashed when I get to the top of a peak as high as this one, but on this occasion I had enough energy to help Mike build us a rock shelter to protect us from the wind as soon as we got to the top. That used to be unheard of in my case, but not any longer. And no altitude sickness! I was very surprised how good I was feeling up there. I am just glad that I did not have to consume as much water as Mike did the previous night. I did however stick to his rule about drinking plenty of fluids during the hike. I am sure that was a huge factor as to why I did so well.

Me and Grizzly Adams on top of Colorado with that "towering, huge, enormous" mountain out in the distance behind us.

We advertised this climb in our Hughes hiking club newsletter, but there were no takers. Mike and I were the only ones in our club crazy enough to do something like this I guessed. Once at the top, Mike surprised me by awarding me with a highpointers tee-shirt and two 'five peaks' patches. One patch was from our company's hiking club "The HAC Packers" for climbing five 'peaks of the month' (which this peak was), and the other patch was for hiking five highpoints as a member of the Highpointers Club. This was my sixth highpoint, but Mike made sure I got the patch regardless. Anybody would be honored to have a friend like Mike. I know I was and still am to this very day. I was actually waiting for him to pull out a Subway sandwich, but that was wishful thinking.

On the way back down to the car, he pointed over to Mount Massive and said, "Look at that gargantuan mountain over there. It's gigantic!"

"It sure is." I responded. "They should call it Mount Massive or something like that."

"How's it goin' eh!?"

After Mount Elbert, we drove down to Colorado Springs and bagged one of Colorado's 53 other 14.000 foot mountains: Pikes Peak, which stands at 14,115 feet and is Colorado's 30th highest mountain. It was pretty cool (literally) as there was a good road all of the way to the top. Too bad Elbert wasn't like this one. I remember getting out of the car and running to the visitor center because it was so cold and windy. I only made it about half way when I had to drop down to my knees to catch my breath. I totally forgot how high we were. Mike came walking up behind me laughing and said, "What's wrong? A little too high for you? HA HA HA!!!"

After driving back down the mountain, we headed straight back to the Denver Hilton for a peaceful, relaxing night before our flight home the next morning. OK, it wasn't the Hilton... OK, we slept on the floor in the airport. Boy, I'll never do that again; famous last words, right? On the way to the airport, we planned out our next climb up in the Pacific Northwest. I knew this next mountain was going to be very challenging, but a lot of fun and very rewarding as well. One thing that I did not realize is that it would be teaching me some valuable lessons in preparation, stress, fear, and in anxiety. I did not really understand or know what anxiety was at the time, but I was about to be slapped across the face with it… Hard!

I always kept the Highpointers Club informed of my progress. After my successful climb in Colorado, the very next issue of their quarterly newsletter included the following: "If you've only got 6HPs, and CA/AZ/NV and CO are 4 of 'em, you're doing it right John White!"

Chapter 6
- Be Mentally Prepared

Oregon Mount Hood Attempt # 1
11,239' May, 1994

All of the other climbers had arrived in Portland, Oregon earlier in the day, and had already gone up to the mountain to prepare for the climb. I flew alone on a later flight, so Mike and another guy, Steven, came back down to pick me up from the airport. Steven had his duffel bag stolen right off the baggage return when they arrived earlier that day, so he came back with Mike to see if it had been recovered. Unfortunately it had not, so he had to go back home from there because he lost all his equipment. Mike and I drove back up to the mountain to Timberline Lodge where we met up with the others. Timberline Lodge is where all of the outdoor shots of *The Shining* were filmed; A very cool and beautiful place.

From Timberline Lodge, we were all taken in a snowcat to a place called Silcox Hut about a mile up the mountain. A snowcat is basically a vehicle that is designed to move on snow and ice. It is about the size of a full-sized truck or van, and has tracks like a tractor or an army tank. Whenever I think of a snowcat, I always think of that one scene in *The Shining* when Jack tells Wendy, "Wendy? You have a big surprise coming to you. Go check out the snowcat and you'll see what I mean. Go check it out! HA HA HA! Go check it out!" God I love that movie, as if you couldn't already tell by now.

I don't know how the driver found this place through the fierce storm that was blowing outside, but he did. All nine of us were packed in that thing very tightly as it made its slow, steady crawl up to the hut. I was one of the unfortunate ones who sat in the back. When the snowcat started climbing, everybody slid back into me, squishing me into the back door that I was praying wouldn't fly open sending me tumbling back down the mountain. Melting snow was also dripping all over me though holes in the rusted roof.

In the snowcat on the way up the mountain

It was during this ride that I started to wonder if I had bitten off a little more than I could chew. All of my mountains to date were fairly easy hikes and climbs. Here I was now on a glacier covered volcano with crevasses, where numerous people had died trying to do the same exact thing I was going to be doing within hours. This is where I first experienced anxiety; or at least I thought it was anxiety. There was a shortness of breath, a tightening of the chest, mixed in with some fear, nervousness, worry, and doubt. I did not like this feeling at all, but I tried to shrug it off every time it reared its ugly head. I would always try and think about something else, but that proved very difficult with the imminent climb looming just a few short hours away. When planning this trip, I felt 100% certain that I would be able to complete it; now I felt as if it had an uncertain outcome.

When we arrived at the entrance to the hut, I was the first to fall out the back of the snowcat and go inside. This place was not only beautiful, but very cool as well. It was built into the side of the mountain. Ultimately, this place made my whole trip worth it. The caretakers of the hut were great people and they served us up a huge dinner of lasagna that evening. We had a raging fire going in the fireplace, snow blowing outside and hot chocolate on tap. We planned on starting our climb at 2:00AM that next morning, so we tried the best we could to get some sleep. We all slept in a bunk room with about eight 'cubbies' with four bunk beds per 'cubby'. The bunk room was carved right into the side of the mountain, and the walls were actually natural rock. We were also the first group to ever rent the place out.

We awoke at 1:00AM to prepare for the climb. This was the first time I ever had to put on so much gear for a peak. As soon as we walked out into the storm which was much worse now, my crampons fell off. Crampons are long spikes that attach to the bottom of your boots for traction in the ice and snow. I tried putting them back on, but everyone started heading up the mountain without me. I decided I would put them on when we got to our first rest stop. The snow on the ground was literally ice, so I was slip-sliding all over the place. It was very slow-going for me and I quickly found myself at the back of the pack. Because of the anxiety I had been experiencing the previous evening, coupled with the fact that I knew I would be holding the group back, I started to have even more doubts and worries about completing this climb.

Geared up and ready to go

I was so unbelievably unprepared for this climb. Not only with my mind-set, but I also didn't have the proper equipment. I didn't think of bringing goggles, so I was being blinded by the frozen rain and snow that was pelting my eyeballs. I also had a cheap faux leather balaclava on my head and around my face (a type of face protection somewhat similar to a ski mask). This thing got absolutely soaked by all the snow and rain blowing around. It didn't have a hole for my mouth, so I was basically sucking the front of it into my mouth as I was trying to get air into my lungs. Being a little stressed about being on a dangerous mountain in the middle of the night, during a blinding snow

58

storm that seemed to be worsening the higher we got, slip sliding all over the place, sucking that damn thing into my mouth so I couldn't breathe properly, and to top it all off, I had a state exam I had to take the following week that I was already totally stressed out about... I gave up. I can still remember the exact moment when this happened; right as I caught up with the others.

I was the last person to arrive at our first planned rest stop. Most everybody had already been there for a good time and were already rested up and starting to leave. I had to make the decision to either continue on with the climb, or quit. It didn't take me long to choose the latter. I was so embarrassed and ashamed of myself when I announced to the two remaining people that I was turning back. I was pretty upset with myself, but I could not continue on. I especially didn't want to hold back anybody, which was already beginning to happen. One of the two guys remaining also took the opportunity to turn back as well, but for different reasons. The third guy who was our leader tried talking us out of our decisions, but we were pretty set; at least I was. The three of us hiked back down to the hut, and then the leader headed back up the mountain to rejoin the team.

When I got inside, I had an inch of ice encrusted around me. The lanyard attached to my ice-ax was as stiff as a board. I took off all of my gear, took a warm shower, crawled into my sleeping bag and began to wonder if I had made the right decision or not. What were these awful feelings I was experiencing? I had never had these feelings before. On top of everything else, was it also because I didn't want to endanger my life for a stupid dream? Was it because I was married and had a beautiful son with another child on the way? Maybe it was a little bit of everything all mixed together. The more I thought about it, the more I realized that I had made the right decision for myself that night as I slowly drifted off to sleep.

It couldn't have been more than thirty minutes later when the door to the hut flew open and the entire team came inside. Snow was swirling into the hut as the last two guys in forced the door closed. I popped up and asked what had happened. They said that the storm got so bad that they had to start digging snow caves for shelter. They also said they came across other climbers already hunkered down in their caves. After a short time of digging, they made the decision to come back down to the hut and try again the following night. Now I knew for a fact that I had made the right decision. Not just for what I experienced, but for safety sake as well. It wasn't long before I was in a deep peaceful sleep again.

The next morning the storm was showing no signs of letting up, and I still knew that I wanted no part of this madness. During breakfast, I made arrangements with the staff to get me off the mountain. I also called the airlines to change my flight. When I called Anna to let her know of my situation, she immediately agreed with my decision and couldn't wait for me to get home. She was seven months pregnant and wanted me to be with her. I hated the fact that I was quitting, especially after how far I had come, but I knew in my heart that I was doing the right thing. I so looked forward to getting home to my family. The other members of the team tried in vain to get me to stay, but my mind was made up. I just wanted to get home.

Later that night when I walked through the front door to my house, Anna was right there with Zachary and greeted me with lots of hugs and kisses. They were very glad that I was home safe. I had only been gone a couple of days, but the situation I got myself into up there did make her a little nervous. She held on to me for a long while, then looked me in the eyes and asked if I was through with mountain climbing. My response was, "I don't know. I don't think so." She had no response to that and gave me another hug. I was really glad to be home and didn't want to think about highpointing anymore; at least not for the time being.

Two months after my failed attempt on Mount Hood, my little girl Caitlyn was born, and then I almost died a few months after that. 1994 was an extreme year for me:

- January – The Northridge Earthquake, which ultimately forced us to leave our home because it was deemed unsafe to live in.
- May – My failed attempt on Mount Hood.
- July – Caitlyn was born.
- October – I contracted Viral Spinal Meningitis and Encephalitis.

I don't remember very much from my bout with Viral Spinal Meningitis and Encephalitis. I remember not feeling well one day and Anna taking me to the hospital. I also remember recovering at home after the worst of it was over. I don't remember much of anything else for the few terrible weeks in between. The stories I heard from Anna about those few weeks were pretty bad, and my doctor later told me that he was really surprised that I had lived through the ordeal.

I was out of work for a few months because of my illness. It was also during this time that Mike called asking if I wanted to get some more peaks with him. I was extremely weak both in body and spirit and was not in the mood to do anything like this. I told him that I probably would not be able to do it and to go without me. He said that he really wanted me to join him this trip, and that he would postpone it for a few months to see how I would be feeling then... so I agreed. I talked to my family about it, and out of concern for me, they were very against it. The one important thing I learned from 1994 was that there is nothing more important in life than my health and my family, and I had no plans of putting either of them back into jeopardy ever again. What an unpleasant time of my life that was. I would have to have a good talk with Mike about the trip before I undertook anything like that. I definitely had a different outlook on life at that moment in time. Looking back, I consider 1994 to be one of the worst years of my life. The only thing that made it all worth it was my beautiful baby girl Caitlyn coming into my life.

As for the state exam I was all stressed out about? I aced it.

Chapter 7
- An Unwanted Finale

A couple months after my failed attempt on Hood, I was back to work, my strength was coming back, and I was starting to feel pretty good physically. I had been thinking about this trip with Mike the whole time since he called, and focused on making myself stronger so I could do it with him. It was going to be a fairly simple trip and I was finally able to talk my family into the idea. I told Mike the good news one afternoon after work, and we immediately got together and planned out the whole trip within an hour. We planned on doing 14 peaks in a matter of just five days. It was going to basically be all of the states in the southeast from the Mississippi River to the Atlantic Ocean; and from the Gulf of Mexico to the Mason Dixon Line. All of them were going to be simple drive-ups and short effortless hikes. The most highpoints I had ever done in one trip were the two back in Georgia and Tennessee. Now I was going to do 14 including Georgia and Tennessee again, and I was finally going to get Sassafras Mountain in South Carolina. This was all a little bit of idiocy on my part, but I was excited and ready to go anyway.

Missouri Taum Sauk Mountain
1,172' March 4, 1995

I don't know if everybody experiences this, but when I hear certain songs, it takes me back to a place and time where I vividly remember where I was, and what I was doing while listening to that particular song. This was one of those times. Whenever I hear "Hotel California" by *The Eagles*, it takes me back to driving down that lonely, dark, forested road in the middle the night leading to Missouri's highest mountain.

Mike was working at the time as a realtor at Realty World in the South Bay. He had brought along his large, magnetic door signs that he stuck onto the doors of the rental car before we departed for the mountain. The guy at the car rental agency gave us the strangest look as we took off out of the parking lot. We crossed the Mississippi River within minutes of leaving the airport, which would be the first of many crossings of this great river in the upcoming years. We had officially started on our next great highpointing adventure.

I always made sure to read the guidebook before each climb, and I took the opportunity to do just that while Mike was doing the driving. I had noticed that there were some warnings regarding this highpoint that I failed to recognize during the planning of this trip back home. The book stated that this mountain was located on private property, the owner didn't take to kindly to trespassers, and he had guard dogs that the author quoted as being, "vicious and loud". I started to freak out a little upon reading this and immediately shared the information with Mike, to which he promptly responded, "We didn't come all this way to turn back. We're going to get this peak one way or another".

"Well, I really don't think we should do it, at least not tonight."

"Why?"

"Because this guy doesn't sound very friendly and either do his dogs."

Mike was quiet for a bit, and then said, "You know how cold it is outside?"

"No."

"About twenty degrees. Do you really think this guy is going to leave his dogs outside in the cold like this? He probably has them locked up inside somewhere."

"I don't know. Do you really want to take that chance?"

He paused a bit more, then said, "Well, OK. I'll tell you what: let's at least get up there and assess the situation. If it doesn't seem right, we'll wait 'till morning and come up with a new game plan."

"OK. That sounds good to me. I just don't want to run into any trouble."

"Agreed."

I didn't know what we were going to do once we got up there. Were we going to sneak onto his property in the middle of the night? What if we were attacked by his dogs? It was a dark, moonless night, the temperature was well below freezing, and we were in very unfamiliar territory. I was starting to have some feelings like what I had experienced up on Mount Hood the previous year. I hated the way it made me feel, and I was also starting to feel a little sick to my stomach as well. I felt just awful and I had never really felt that way before I started highpointing. This was all supposed to be fun! I was starting to think that I was getting myself back into a bad situation again. I really wasn't mentally prepared to go commando like Mike always seemed to be. I tried to get the right mindset, but those feelings always took over.

We found the small, windy road that would lead us to the top of the mountain. I was worried beyond belief that we were going to have a run-in with the property owner. As we continued up the thick, forested road, I told Mike to turn off the headlights and drive just using the running lights as I kept a keen eye out for this guy's house. I told Mike to drive slowly so we wouldn't wake him or his dogs. We never saw a house, and when we got to the end of the road, we found a modern parking lot and a sign that said, "Welcome to Taum Sauk Mountain State Park". What the hell? Mike and I looked at each other and both shouted out a loud "WOOO HOOOooo!!!" at the same time. What a huge relief that was. Everything I was feeling went away in an instant.

It was a very short walk to the summit from the parking lot, and the walk was vastly different than I had imagined earlier with a crazy man and his dogs chasing us through the dark woods. It was extremely cold and pitch-black when we got to the top. I was wearing a light jacket and no gloves. By the time I reached the top, I was wishing I had brought a down parka, long johns and some gloves. I had to keep moving just to stay warm. Being a true California boy, this was my first real cold experience. One would think that my experience on Mount Hood would have been much colder, but this was not the case. This was a different kind of cold, a cold that went right through to my bones. And the fact that I was not dressed properly just compounded the issue.

Another highpointing tradition of mine was that I always wore the same jacket to each peak. Steamy hot or freezing cold, it was always there with me one way or another. In this case it just wasn't quite enough. I always made sure there were distinguishable landmarks in the pictures unique to each peak whenever I had my photo taken on the summits. In this case on Taum Sauk Mountain, it was a granite plaque mounted in the ground near a large rock. I tried to brush the snow off the plaque, but it was covered with about ¼ inch of ice. I tried scraping the ice with the edges of my shoes and then with a stick, but it was no use. It was frozen solid. I really wanted to see what the plaque said, and I wanted it in my picture.

Mike said, "Hey! You want that ice off there? No problem! Step aside."

He stepped up to the marker, unzipped his fly, and proceeded to melt the ice in a way that only a guy could do with any degree of accuracy. Afterward, he stepped back to admire his work and said with a smile, "How's it goin' eh!?" With that I whipped out my book, flag and camera, and I was in business.

I usually kept my book and flag in a Ziploc bag to help prevent them from damage and moisture. Sometimes we hiked in the rain and snow, and I wanted to keep them dry and protected forever. I opened the Ziploc bag to get them out for the photo, and because my hands were absolutely frozen solid, I accidentally dropped everything thing right into the snow. The book fell out of the bag and got buried, and the bag completely filled with the white powdery stuff. Mike almost fell down because he was laughing so hard. When he finally stopped, he asked me, "Hey John! Why do you keep your book in a Ziploc bag? Is it to keep it dry?! HA HA!" We still laugh about that one from time to time.

As we were walking back down to the car, Mike came up with a wacky idea that we try and do as many peaks as we could within a 24 hour period. I asked if he was serious, and he gave me his famous wide-eyed grin that is somewhat like the Cheshire Cat from *Alice in Wonderland*; very wide and very toothy. I have learned that when he gives a smile like that, it's game time. I asked when and where we were going to get any decent sleep. He said, "In the car as the other person drives." That's all I needed to hear; I was in. It was about 12:15AM, when we got back to the car. I threw my book and bag up onto the dash so they would dry-out as we made our way to Indiana.

I wasn't expecting too much excitement driving through the Missouri countryside at 1:00AM. I also wasn't paying any attention to my speed as I was clocked going 75 in a 45. The patrol car was just another vehicle passing us in the opposite direction on a lonely road in the middle of the night. He turned on all his lights as he passed us and spun his car around behind me. This scared the hell out of me, and I think my heart skipped a beat or two. Mike was fast asleep.

"Mike!... Mike!... We're being pulled over!"

"Huh? What?" Mike stuttered half asleep.

"We're being pulled over! Wake up."

The Trooper of course wanted to know what the big hurry was… so we told him. After the look of total bewilderment left his face, he asked for my driver's license. I gave him my license as well as my three California good driver extensions.

"What the heck are these?" he asked.

"Driver's license extensions." I replied.

"Driver's license 'whats-its'?!" he exclaimed.

I explained to him what they were, as he looked at me with a puzzled face that I'll never forget. He handed everything back to me, told me to keep within the speed limits, and let us go. Mike said he probably did that because:

- I was a Californian.
- I was driving a car registered in Tennessee.
- There were magnetic door signs advertising a business almost two thousand miles away.
- We were on the back roads of Missouri.
- We were climbing mountains in the middle of the night.
- We were on our way to Indiana to get our next mountain.
- There was a half asleep, crazy looking guy sitting next to me wrapped up in a sleeping bag.

Lucky for us, he probably just didn't want to deal with the paperwork.

Indiana Hoosier Hill
1,257' March 4, 1995

After crossing the Mississippi River for the second time on this trip, we were now headed due east through Illinois and Indiana. Driving through this part of the country was a different experience for me; it was strange looking out at the barren, dormant land, but at the same time being absolutely and utterly frozen. Frozen grass, frozen trees, frozen lakes and rivers, frozen roads, and frozen people everywhere.

After being in the same clothes for two days, I decided it was time to change into something that smelled a little nicer; at least my shirt anyway. We pulled off Interstate 70 in Terre Haute and parked at a Chick-fil-A. I wanted to get out of the car to stretch a little as well as change my shirt. I opened the door, got out, then immediately jumped back into the car slamming the door shut behind me. It was FREAKING COLD! Really?! How do these people put up with this? I still had to get a clean shirt out of the trunk, so I went back out into icy air, got a shirt and decided just to change it right there on the spot. It was so cold I thought one of my nipples fell off right there in the parking lot. You never saw a person change a shirt and get back into a car so fast. Mike just sat there in the warm car laughing until it was his turn. When he got out of the car to change his shirt, I looked back and noticed all of the people in the chicken-joint were pointing and laughing at us. They continued to stare even as we drove away. I guess we were Indiana's entertainment for the day.

We got back on the interstate and drove across Indiana until we found our turnoff just short of the Ohio state line. The road we took leading north from the interstate turned out to be rather enjoyable for the last ten miles because it was much like a roller coaster. Mike broke from protocol and actually sped up on this portion of the road. When we arrived at the peak, it was sunny, totally clear, and about 10:00AM. The golden grass was gently blowing in the breeze, and the trees hiding the summit had a stark, leafless beauty about them. I opened the door, got out, then immediately jumped back into the car slamming the door shut behind me again. It was FREAKING COLD! Really!? It was so cold I thought my *other* nipple fell off! I am a Southern California boy, and not used to this kind of weather at all. I thought to myself that people that lived in that part of the country must really be a tough breed for sure.

My guidebook stated that the peak was about a fifty yard walk west from the road. I started counting off the yards as we walked away from the car through the crunchy, frozen grass, "One... two... three... four... five... six... seven... here we are!" It was a good thing I was looking off into the woods as we were walking and saw the marker just to the right of us. Fifty yards? We would have ended up deep in the woods looking for this thing for hours. This wouldn't be the first time my book wasn't very accurate. We had to climb an icy metal ladder over a barbed wire fence to get to the marker that waited for us just on the other side. This was peak #2 in our 24 hour peak-bagging quest. When I signed the register, I noticed that the previous entry stated that they (a couple) had sex on the marker just the day before. I was very impressed that they did something like this when it was so FREAKING COLD! When we got back to the car, I noticed that about five hundred feet away there was a rise next to the road. We went over to check it out, and it too claimed to be Indiana's highpoint. We took pictures there also; just in case. Better safe than sorry.

This peak was rather unremarkable as it didn't really seem like a peak at all and didn't have much to offer. This was the first of several highpoints that I really couldn't tell was an actual highpoint because it was flat and looked like everything else around it. On peaks like Indiana's, I just had to trust in science as well as my trusty guidebook that got me there. We finished up in a hurry, and were now off to Ohio. I wasn't really expecting anything much different there after our exciting Indiana experience.

48 Mountains

Ohio Campbell Hill
1,550' March 4, 1995

It wasn't quite as cold as Indiana, but the terrain in Ohio was very similar: flat.

Instead of the summit being located way out in the country like all of my previous highpoints, this one was located on the grounds of the cleverly named Ohio Hi-Point Career Center. The summit was right next to the school's parking lot and was marked with a flag pole and a couple of park benches. I had been used to stunning views after hours of strenuous hiking, and the ones in the mid-west were starting to get a little on the boring side. I briefly thought back to when my dad had said "You have *got* to be kidding me!" after we had reached Georgia's highpoint. It didn't take much for me to imagine what he would be saying about Middle America's summits.

This was Peak #3 in our 24 hour quest, and I was glad that Mike had come up with this idea because there was no reason to stay on these peaks any longer than it took to take our photos. When we got back to the car, Mike had me take a promo-picture of him next to our now extremely filthy vehicle showing his Realty World magnetic door signs with the Ohio highpoint in the background. Afterward, I took one of the signs off to see just how dirty our car was, and the giant rectangular sparkling clean white patch said it all. Mike took a picture of that as well and later told me that his boss back in California really got a kick out of the photos.

We jumped back in the car and were now off to Pennsylvania. I hoped there would be a little more adventure than on our previous two peaks. Before I knew it, we were crossing the border into West Virginia. I got out my camera to take a photo, and we crossed over into Pennsylvania before I had a chance to shoot a single picture.

Pennsylvania Mount Davis
3,213' March 4, 1995

Driving to this peak was kind of interesting and eerie at the same time. It was now about 7:00PM and extremely dark outside as we neared the summit. We had to drive north from Maryland to just inside of Pennsylvania where we would find the mountain. We soon found ourselves travelling slowly down old, narrow, dark country roads through Amish country. The snow continued getting deeper the higher up the mountain we drove, and we just kept plowing through it the best we could until we finally got the car stuck about one half mile from the summit. Mike asked, "Now what?", and I suggested that we leave the car right where it was and walk the final distance to the peak. We were on a mission, and we didn't need matters like this slowing us down.

"Well, what if somebody wants to get by?"

"Mike, there's nobody else, dim-witted like us, trying to get to the peak… this late at night… in the snow. Believe me, we're the only ones up here doing this tonight. We'll be OK. Let's just leave it here and get going. We will be up and back in no time."

"Well, there might be, and I don't want anybody messing with our car."

With that, he put the car in reverse and attempted to back it off the road so others could pass if they wanted too. He didn't get very far because we were stuck!

"Let's just go get the peak," I suggested. "We'll deal with this when we get back."

Mike reluctantly agreed and we walked the final distance to the top.

Except for the snow, this was a very easy peak to complete. I couldn't figure out why, but there was nobody else up there but us; much like Ohio, Indiana and Missouri. This was Peak #4 in our 24 hour quest. The book was wrong again as to where the actual highpoint was, but we were able to find it within minutes not far from where the book said it was. Once there, I saw a huge boulder nearby that was definitely higher than what the book stated was the highpoint; which was the sign. I walked up

to the boulder and noticed that it had a USGS Benchmark*
cemented onto the top of it. There was no benchmark by the
sign, so I concluded that the rock was the actual highpoint. Just
to be sure though, we had our photos taken at both locations.
Afterwards, we hiked back down to the car to begin our trek to
our next highpoint in Maryland. There was no time to dilly-dally
as we were on a mission, and there was nothing that spectacular
keeping us up there just like on the previous few peaks.

Once we got back down to the car, we were once again
faced with the fact that the car was still basically stuck in place.
I immediately started to dig out the snow from behind one of the
tires when Mike stopped me and suggested that he should first
try backing it up again. He got in, started the car, popped it in
reverse, and we were free! As mike backed away from the spot
where the car was stuck, there was a perfect rectangle of melted
snow where the car was parked. Our hot car had basically
melted the snow thus freeing us while we were up on the
mountain! I jumped in very happy that we didn't have to spend
any wasted time digging snow away from the car. Mike then
proceeded to back down the road staying in the tracks we made
on the way up until we found a good spot to get turned around.
It was times like these that added some adventure to what we
were doing.

After we got off the mountain, we stopped at a local
McDonald's for dinner before we hit the main road to our next
peak. This is where the famous "Maryland McDonald's Ten
Cent Incident" took place. Mike got into an argument with a
poor girl behind the counter because he wanted two double
cheeseburgers without cheese and she didn't understand what he
was asking for, or why he was asking for something so out of
the norm. I told her that he wanted two double hamburgers, and
he said, "No! I want two double cheeseburgers without cheese!"

"Why?!" I asked.

He pointed to a poster on the wall and said, "Because there is a special today on double cheeseburgers, and they are ten cents cheaper than hamburgers, and I don't want any cheese."

I stood there and looked at him for a moment, looked at the girl and shrugged my shoulders, then walked off to get us a table. When I sat down and began to eat, I noticed that a few other customers in the place were all quietly eating and watching Mike as he continued to explain to the girl what it was he wanted. The manager finally got involved and told her to do exactly what he was asking her to do. All that for a dime, but you have to know and understand Mike the way I do. He is very affluent and says he is so because of things like this. I couldn't help but to start giggling out loud which made some others sitting near me start as well. That was too funny.

Leaving Ohio's highpoint earlier in the day, I had wished for a little more adventure which I did get with the snow in Pennsylvania and the "Ten Cent Incident", but this day's adventures were just beginning and things were about to get a little spooky and very scary.

A USGS Benchmark is a survey monument which is usually a bronze disk about four inches in diameter set in rock or a permanent structure. There are millions of these located all across America, but the ones that were most important to me were the 48 located on top of my highpoints. These mark the actual highpoints, and show information such as elevation and the date it was placed there. Most of them were very easy to find, while others were never found. It was never my priority to locate these, just to stand on top of the summits.

Maryland Backbone Mountain
3,360 March 4, 1995

I tried to get some shuteye during the short drive from 'Ten Cent' McDonald's to Backbone Mountain, so I put in a tape I had made to relax me a bit. Just a of couple months prior, during my first week back to work after my illness, I was sitting alone in my car waiting for a training class to begin. It was a cold, drizzly, gray day which seemed to fit perfect for the way I was feeling at the time; I was still very weak, and also somewhat nervous about being back to work. I had the radio dialed in to some obscure station that started playing a song that I had never heard before. It was beautiful and seemed to immediately console and take me to another place of total ease. The song was "Little suicides" by *The Golden Palominos*; I purchased the CD later that evening on my way home from work. I was to join Mike on our road trip in a couple of months, so I copied all of my favorite songs onto a cassette for the trip, including a few from my new CD. "Little suicides" is still on my playlist to this day. The last thing I remember just before falling asleep to my music was Mike ejecting my tape and tuning the radio to a classical music station which completely finished the job and knocked me totally out for the duration.

Just like the four previous mountains on this day-long spree, this mountain was going to be one of the easiest peaks of the entire trip. Mike and I were really looking forward to another easy one so we could continue on with our 24 hour pursuit. According to the guidebook, all we needed to do was to follow a gravel logging road for about a mile that would take us all the way to the top. This was really going to be a cinch.

When we turned onto the road leading to the peak, we were immediately faced with a bullet riddled, hand-painted sign that read:

Highpointers
KEEP OUT!

Mike skidded to a stop right in front of the sign which immediately woke me out of my slumber. As the dust slowly drifted away, our headlights fully illuminated the warning which was obviously directed right at us. Now what were we going to do? I looked over to Mike and suggested that we drive up to the top anyway. It was late, and who would catch us if we kept it quiet. Mike got a little freaked out about that idea. "What if we get caught?" he asked.

"In the middle of the night?!" I shot back. "Come on, let's go up. We didn't come all this way for nothing."

"I don't know…"

"Look at you? Last night you were all gung-ho about climbing Missouri; now you are being totally cautious."

Mike just sat there staring past the sign up the road.

"Listen: just drive real slow and quiet. We will be up and out in no time".

He just kept sitting there quietly not saying anything.

"If we hike to the top, it will take us about twenty minutes each way. I'll bet you right now that it will take over an hour to get up and back to the car if we hike it. And then we will barely have enough time to get West Virginia's peak within the 24 hours."

"We'll have enough time if we hike it. Let's just hide the car somewhere and get going."

I let out a sigh and said, "Alright, but let's try to do this quickly. We're running out of time."

We really didn't need this setback because we needed to make up some time due to getting stuck in the snow in Pennsylvania. We figured that our next peak in West Virginia would be the final mountain of our 24 hour quest, but in my opinion those hopes were slowly starting to fade. Mike drove the car down the highway a little ways, and found an old, unused dirt road that was a perfect place to stash the car and start our covert hike. After he parked the car, I opened the door and stepped up to my ankles in mud. I almost lost a shoe in the muck when I pulled my foot out. This really pissed me off as we had no time for setbacks. I immediately put on my hiking boots, threw my muddy shoes in the back seat of the car and we started our hike.

We quickly found a trail leading up towards the peak through the thick, dark woods. The trail was an old, overgrown, rutted road with fresh rainfall flowing down the middle of it. Sometimes the whole road was flowing with inch deep water and made for a difficult trek. It was so dark and there were so many trees that we couldn't see the summit let alone the trail we were walking on. We eventually came upon a good gravel road about halfway up the mountain that we figured was the original road with the "KEEP OUT" sign posted on it down below. Mike took a couple minutes to build a small rock cairn on the side of the road so we would know where to turn off on our way back down.

We followed the road up the mountain until it came to an abrupt end at some snow covered trees. This is where we would have parked the car if we drove up. We were obviously not on top of the mountain yet and we couldn't find a trail anywhere. We continued cross-country, the whole time going uphill towards the obvious ridgeline. We knew it was up there somewhere. We were going over and under logs, slipping off of rocks and 'post-holing' through the snow up to our knees trying to find the highpoint. Mike kept asking if we were going in the right direction, and my response was always, "Yes. We need to get to the highpoint which means we need to keep going up," so that's what we did.

Sometimes the terrain sort of leveled off and we had to figure out which way was still up. It was starting to get frustrating, and it was still absolutely pitch black. All of a sudden I bumped my head right into a frozen, metal pole holding up a sign marking the highpoint. "Found it!" There I was standing on the summit of peak #5 in a 24 hour period. It was about 11:00PM which meant that we still had two hours to get to the next peak in West Virginia. Peak #6 was still within our grasp at this point, but barely.

We took our photos and started back down the mountain. A comment about taking flash photos when your eyes are fully adjusted to pitch black: The flash is so intense that it almost knocks you off of your feet. You can actually see the wave of light as it leaves the camera and comes straight towards you. Then afterward you really can't see anything for several seconds. As we left the highpoint, we found a very good trail that took us back to the exact same point where the gravel road ended. It was about two feet from where we went cross-country. "Arrgh! Really!?" We made our way back down the road to Mike's cairn, and we started down the muddy, wet trail back to the car.

It was about halfway down the mountain when I thought I saw a faint flicker of light out of the corner of my right eye. I stopped for a moment and stared back through the thick, pitch-black woods, but never saw anything. I started walking again and just as I caught back up to Mike, I thought I saw it again.

"Mike, stop a second. I thought I saw something."

"What?"

"I don't know. It looked like a flashlight or something way out in the woods."

We stood there for a moment and stared out into the woods, but there was nothing.

"You're seeing things. Come-on, let's go."

Just then I saw it again and it seemed a little closer this time. I quietly told Mike to stop, and we both looked back into the woods.

"I don't see anything." Mike said sternly. "Will you knock it off? You're starting to creep me out!"

"Mike. Look." as I pointed out in the general direction of the light. "There it is again."

We both stared for a moment in total silence as we looked out into the darkness; then there it was. About two hundred yards out through the trees we saw what appeared to be somebody walking in our general direction with a flashlight. This immediately sent chills up my spine and I could feel my adrenaline start to pump and the hair on my arms start to rise.

"Who is that?" I asked.

"How the hell do I know? Let's get outta here!" Mike responded in a loud whisper.

We started walking at a much quicker pace now, which was difficult because of the muddy, slippery conditions. I kept looking back into the woods and seeing that ghostly light flickering out in the distance. Every time I looked back, I would lose my footing and almost slip and fall. After a short while, we stopped to see if we could still see anything. Sure enough there it was, and it looked as if it had changed direction and was now headed straight for us. It still appeared to be about two hundred yards out. We were now taking this thing very seriously. We continued down the mountain stopping every once in a while to look through the trees to see if it was still out there. Sure enough, it was always out there and heading straight towards us. The light was obviously on the same trail and was doing a pretty good job keeping up with our hurried pace.

I have never been scared like that before in my life and felt such relief when we made it back to the car. I had my keys out way before we got to the car just to make sure our getaway would be that much quicker. I looked back but didn't see the light any longer, and this really freaked me out because now I didn't know where this person was. I had never been pursued by a total stranger before, and it was very scary and nerve-racking. We both jumped into the car with our muddy boots still on, and left burn-out marks on the road as we left. Mike and I laugh about it now, but talk about spooky. The only thing I could come up with is that it was the guy who put up the sign telling us to stay out. I also had to assume that if it was the landowner, then he most-likely had a weapon or why else would he be pursuing us so quickly in the middle of the night in pitch black, in the rain. And thank goodness we didn't take the car up like I had suggested before the climb. Whoever this person was, he for certain would have heard our car on our way up and who knows what the outcome would have been then. I never wanted to go through something like that again. No more hiking on private property for me. Never again.

Later that year, I read in our club newsletter that the landowner had contacted the club and made it official that the highpoint was closed and closed for good. He also stated that trespassers would be dealt with severely. I believe that whole heartedly after what I had experienced. Looking back, I am glad we were able to get this peak, but I would never do anything like that again. Mike now tells the story as if we were being pursued by the CIA being so near to Washington D.C. and all. At least we were now safely off to West Virginia, but making it our sixth peak in 24 hours just wasn't meant to be. It didn't matter much anymore as we were getting pretty tired and just wanted this day to be over.

West Virginia Spruce Knob
4,863' March 5, 1995

We got the car stuck in the snow for the second time that day. This time we were only about five hundred feet from the peak and it was 1:00AM. That was it. West Virginia would not be our sixth peak in the 24 hour period and we were so damn close. After we got stuck, we had to get out of the car and change into our winter gear in blizzard-like conditions. This time we left the car where it got stuck. There was no way anybody else was as stupid as us and would be coming up there that night. We hiked the final distance and arrived at the peak at 1:30AM. We just missed it by one lousy hour. We didn't get our six peaks in 24 hours, but we did get five. And we did get all six in a 25 hour period which was a huge achievement in itself. We were pretty proud of ourselves regardless, and now we had the stories to tell.

Like many of the highpoints on this particular trip, there was nothing very special about this one, especially in the middle of the night. There was an observation tower on the top, but instead of climbing it, we took shelter from the elements below it. This is also where we took our photos. Here we were again out in the middle of nowhere, alone, and patting each other on the back for our huge success. Afterward, we quickly headed back down to the car so we could start making our way into Virginia where our next peak awaited.

It was about 2:30AM when we were finally back in the car and on our way to Virginia. I was passed out in the passenger seat while Mike was driving by Braille on a two lane windy road through the Appalachians. He couldn't take any more and woke me to let me know that he had to pull over somewhere to get some sleep or we were going to die. He asked me if I wanted to drive and I said, "No way." He then asked me where we should park, and I said, very tiredly, "I don't care Mike. Pull over anywhere..." He pulled over right there on the spot, and one minute later we were both sound asleep on the side of the road somewhere in Appalachia. The next morning, I awoke to the sun shining straight into my eyes. I started to stretch and looked over to Mike to see if he was still sleeping and he was staring at me with that damn huge wide-eyed grin of his again. Without a word, he started the car, popped it into gear, and we were off.

"How long have you been awake?" I asked.

"For about twenty minutes."

"Why didn't you just start driving while I slept?"

"I didn't want to wake you."

"Thanks. Now can you pull the car back over so I can take a leak?"

"Yeah. I guess I gotta take one too. How's it goin' eh!?"

We were now headed for the grand adventure of Virginia's unforgiving highpoint. This time our woes wouldn't be because we got the car stuck in snow, or didn't get close enough to the trailhead. No. This time we got totally confused, totally lost, and our amazing and long friendship would become regrettably strained for the very first time ever.

Virginia Mount Rogers
5,729' March 5, 1995

We arrived in the early afternoon, and it immediately started to drizzle as soon as we stepped out of the car. This meant that our three hour hike would now take a little longer than anticipated. The guidebook gave very detailed directions on how to reach the summit, and the very first instruction was to go through a gate right down the hill and across the field from the parking lot. I immediately spotted the gate and we were on our way. We passed a sign warning us to be prepared for extreme weather changes, and all I had on was my typical blue jacket. Because the weather was rather nice, I falsely assumed that I was good to go. The guidebook also mentioned that the trail to the peak was marked the entire length with "Blue blazes." These are basically painted markings on rocks. Once you get to one, you should always be able to see the next one further up the trail. These are designed to not only guide you to your destination, but to get you safely back to where you began as well. We never saw any of them; well, not when it mattered anyway.

This mountain had one of the worst trail systems I had ever encountered. There were trails all over the place, and none of them were marked properly, or even marked at all for that matter. I don't know where we ended up, but we somehow hiked right past a turn-off that would have led us straight to the peak. This turn-off wasn't in the book, or marked on the trail. I think we ended up going around the back side of the mountain. It was very hard to tell due to the low clouds and constant rain. After a few hours of searching, we figured that we had walked way too far and should have found the peak by then. Actually, we should had found the peak and been back to the car by then. We doubled back and found another trail that we didn't see on the way up and decided to see where it would take us. We must had walked about a mile on this trail, and lost some five hundred feet in elevation in the process. I told Mike that we were definitely going the wrong way and should turn around. We doubled back to the first place where we doubled back and stopped to assess our situation.

We had now spent about five hours looking for the peak and had no idea where it was. The rain was steadily getting stronger, we didn't really know where we were, and it started getting dark. It was because of these factors that we made the very difficult decision to give up on this mountain and come back some other day in the future to climb it. It wouldn't be happening on this trip.

On the way back down the mountain to the car, we came to an intersection in the trail that we had not seen on the way up. Mike wanted to see where it led to, so he went up to check it out while I waited. He was only gone for a few minutes when I heard him call down to me to come on up to where he was. It turned out to be a trail marked with blue blazes just as the book had described. We followed the trail to a peak that we were 99% certain was the summit, but we really couldn't tell for sure. The mountain was shrouded in thick fog which prevented us from being able to see twenty feet out in any direction. It was a very rocky peak with blue blazes painted everywhere. The photo of the peak in my guidebook showed trees and a sign at the summit, but there were no trees or sign anywhere to be seen. We didn't look very hard though because it was getting dark, a gale force wind had started to blow, and the rain was now falling heavy. I wanted to take photos of us at the top, but our cameras would have most certainly been destroyed by the heavy downpour. We declared that we were in fact standing on the summit and then decided that it was really time to get the hell off the mountain as soon as possible due to the poor conditions. We were soon back down to the main trail and heading back to the car. This mountain turned out to be my only highpoint that I don't have any photo record of.

Now when we had started the hike earlier that day, we went down a gentle, sloping hill to the gate. The gate was probably about three hundred feet in distance from the car, and we had to go through it to continue up the trail to the mountain. Now on the way back down to the car, we came to the exact same gate and proceeded to walk through it again. It was still raining, getting darker, and now starting to get a little cold. We were not prepared for this situation because it was only supposed to be a short three hour hike to the top and back. All we had with us were our daypacks and light jackets that were now totally rain soaked, but at least we were almost back to the car. After we passed through the gate, we walked up the hill towards our car, and we walked… and we walked…

"Mike, I think something is wrong here" I stated.

At that exact moment, my left knee started giving me problems and it became very difficult to walk. This had never happened to me before and it was really painful. I couldn't keep up with Mike who was walking up the hill further and further away from me.

"Mike, we didn't walk this far when we walked from the car to the gate!" I shouted up to him.

He shouted back, "The car is up here somewhere!"

"No it's not!" I shouted back, "We were not parked this far from the gate!"

Mike never heard what I said because he had disappeared over a rise. This was crazy. He was so far ahead of me now that we could not hear each other any longer. I kept yelling to him, "Mike!… Mike!...," but it was no use.

We had been searching for a while now, and I knew we were going in the wrong direction, so I decided it was time to look for some shelter. It was getting colder and darker by the minute, and it was now time to look for somewhere dry to spend the night if we had too. I knew Mike would come back for me sooner or later, but he was still nowhere in sight. I was getting a little nervous, and I'm not embarrassed to say, a little scared as well. I was not mentally prepared for this. I wanted to turn back down the trail to the gate where at least I knew where we were. But what if Mike was right? What if the car *was* in fact up this trail? But I knew the car was not up there and that we were going the wrong way. What if I turned around and found the car, but Mike got lost, or I got lost? This hike had really turned into a messed-up situation that I had never experienced before. I was really starting to get concerned for our safety, and being totally alone, I started feeling what I thought were symptoms of anxiety again; those awful feelings that I somehow kept getting myself into over and over again.

I couldn't find any suitable shelter, so I finally decided to continue up the trail to try and find Mike. I slowly limped up the hill for a long distance and finally did catch up with him after about thirty minutes of searching. He was just standing there with a very puzzled look on his face. I looked around, and at that point noticed that we were back on the top of the mountain where the blue blazes were painted.

"What in the hell's going on here?!" I exclaimed.

This not only meant that we had hiked this mountain twice using two different trails, but also meant that we now had to head back down the mountain, AGAIN, for a second time.

"We really need to get out of here," Mike said.

With that, we decided to go back down the same way we just came up instead of going down the way we had previously as it was a much better trail.

On the way back down the mountain I started to think to myself if all this highpointing stuff was really worth it to me any longer. This was supposed to be a very simple mountain, and look what was happening to us. If we had to stay out there over night, there was a good chance that something very serious could have ensued. We we're not prepared for our situation, and all I could imagine was us dying up there from hypothermia or something. I still had many highpoints 100% tougher than this one yet to do, and that simple mountain in Virginia was trying to do me in. After a lot of thought, I decided that this quest of mine was over. I only had a dozen or so mountains completed at that point, and had already experienced the awful feelings of fear and anxiety on four of them now. These were not very good odds. I was done; this was supposed to be fun! It took me a while to work up the nerve to tell Mike, and he didn't take it very well when I eventually did. He tried talking me out of quitting, but I wouldn't budge. My mind was made up.

We continued walking through the cold, wet darkness and eventually came back to that infamous gate that we had already gone through twice before. We went through it for a third time and there in front of us was the field followed by the gentle, sloping hill leading right up to the car just as I thought. I still don't know how we did it, but we had gone through the same gate three times now, the first two times in the same direction. What a nightmare that all turned out to be. As we walked across the field towards the car, we passed the sign again warning us to be prepared for extreme weather changes. I learned from this never to take these warnings for granted ever again.

We got in the car and started heading to Kentucky. Mike continued trying to get me to change my mind, but I wouldn't have any of it. I could tell he was quite upset with my decision, and he had every right to be. I told him to take me to the nearest airport in either Knoxville, Tennessee or Charlotte, North Carolina so I could fly home from there. He finally came to the realization that I was very serious, and started to work with me on getting me home. He said he would continue the trip without me after he dropped me off, and I was totally fine with that decision.

Since we were so far out of the way from any major city, we eventually agreed to do three more peaks together, and then he would drop me off at my dad's house in Atlanta, Georgia. He would then continue on to do the remaining highpoints from there.

Kentucky Black Mountain
4,145' March 5, 1995

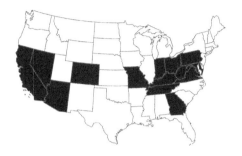

The back country through Virginia and Kentucky late at night was kind of eerie. It is a very dark and lonely part of the country. Not too many cities or towns. The roads are all very goofy as well. The map shows a state highway going from 'point A' to 'point B', but in reality, there are turn-offs everywhere. You have to watch for every road sign you pass to make sure you are still on the correct road and not going to have to turn off somewhere. I missed a turnoff and didn't realize it until I rolled into some town ten miles north of where we were supposed to be. I gently turned the car around to get us back on the correct path. Mike was sleeping and I didn't want him to catch my twenty mile mistake.

When we got to the Kentucky state line, there was a huge coal mine right on the border. I had never seen something so big in my life. There were thousands of lights all over it and it looked like a small city of its own. It kind of looked like Disneyland. We crossed into Kentucky and immediately started climbing into the mountains. The roads were very steep and narrow and it was a little foggy in places. We eventually found the small road that would lead us to the peak, and reached a gate

95

which meant we were within a couple hundred feet from the summit.

I asked Mike to get out and see if the gate was locked. He didn't want to do this for some reason, so I put the car in park, turned off the motor, and got out of the car to check the gate myself. As soon as I reached the gate, Mike turned the car lights off. I thought for a second that he was messing with me. I turned towards the car and said, "OK. Funny", but the lights remained off.

"Can you turn the lights back on please? I can't see a thing."

There was no response. I went back to the car, opened the door and turned the lights back on myself. Mike snapped at me and said that I was going to kill the car battery by leaving the lights on. He reached over and turned them back off again. I told him that it was only going to be for a minute, and the battery would not have a chance to die in that short of time. We argued about this for a short time until I had had enough. I grabbed my book and flag, slammed the car door shut, and proceeded to make my way to the summit in the dark by myself. A thick fog started rolling in almost immediately after I easily found the radio tower on the summit. Mike eventually followed me up and asked if I wanted my photo taken. Because I was still very frustrated about the whole highpointing thing, and now very pissed off at the situation I was in, I permitted him to take the photo, but I didn't bother displaying my book and flag. I didn't really care anymore and still just wanted to get home more than ever now.

After we took our photos, we went back to the car and started making our way off of the mountain. It was so foggy when we left the summit that we couldn't see a thing. I couldn't even see the end of the hood. I had to drive, literally standing out the window so I could see the white line next to the car. Mike had to do the same on the other side. It didn't matter what was in front of us, because we couldn't see. After about thirty minutes, we finally broke through the fog and were now off to North Carolina.

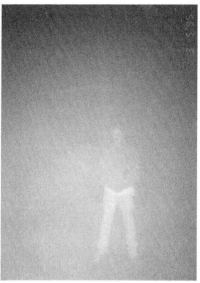

You can barely see my book
sticking out of my left jacket pocket

Later that night when we finally crossed from Virginia into North Carolina, it was about 2:00AM, and was now my turn to drive by Braille. That was the most tired I had ever been driving a car in my life. It was very scary and stupid, and I'll never forget when I dozed off with my eyes wide open, and then awakened in the next lane.

"That's it!"

I pulled off the freeway at the next ramp, drove up a dark dirt road into some North Carolina woods, parked the car and went to sleep. Mike kind of woke up after I turned the car off and asked what was going on. He fell back asleep before I could answer him. There was a crescent moon out which kept it pretty dark, and the howling dogs out in the darkness made me a little uneasy. They seemed to get closer to the car throughout the night, but there was a point when I just couldn't keep my eyes open any longer. I was now done for the day. Basically what we were doing was driving long, twelve hour shifts and it was really starting to affect us.

As soon as the sun started heating up the car the next morning, we were off again. In Mike's mind, he was off to North Carolina. In my mind, I was getting closer to going home.

North Carolina Mount Mitchell
6,684 March 6, 1995

We were supposed to follow Interstate 26 to the Blue Ridge Parkway, turn east, and then head up a short distance to the peak. Mike decided to take a shortcut down a lonely county road that was supposed to save us about thirty minutes. I happily agreed only because it would get me to my dad's place that much quicker. The road soon turned into a rural dirt path that lead us through a pretty poor shanty town, much like the one shown in the movie Deliverance. I kept a watchful eye and carefully listened for any banjos as we slowly passed through.

We were on the west side of the mountain when we started the short-cut, and somehow ended up way east of the mountain when we realized we missed a turn-off somewhere. It would have been a big waste of time to back-track all those miles to try and find the turn-off we needed, so we looked at the map and found our location as well as a new route to the top. When we got to the Blue Ridge Parkway some thirty miles east of where we should had picked it up, there was a sign that read, "Blue Ridge Parkway Closed at Mount Mitchell." Talk about luck. If we hadn't taken this long, "shortcut' by accident, we would have found the closure the hard way.

This was an easy peak to accomplish. Even though it was only about one hundred feet of stairs, it did take me a long time to get to the top because of my knee. It was hurting so bad that I could hardly bear the pain. I just took each step slowly and one at a time. I think it was caused by me sitting for so long in the cramped car in addition to hiking hard back in Maryland and Virginia. Mike sarcastically asked why I was putting myself through the misery if I had given up on highpointing. It was a very good question that I really didn't have an answer for. When I asked him to take my photo, he again asked, "Why?"

"I don't know. Just in case."

"In case of what?"

"I don't know… In case I ever decide to get back into this. I don't want to have to come all the way back here for a stupid photo."

He reluctantly took my picture, and then I took his. Now that this peak was accomplished, it was off to South Carolina and then to my final destination in Atlanta and then home.

Mike and I really hadn't said much to each other since Black Mountain the night before, or even since I told him I was done with highpointing back in Virginia for that matter. It really sucked because we were usually always talking or joking about something, and now it was pretty much just silence. I know he was upset about the decision I made. Heck, I was upset with myself for the decision I made, but I knew at the time it was the right decision and I guess there really wasn't much more to talk about.

South Carolina Sassafras Mountain
3,560' March 6, 1995

There is not really too much to say about this peak, except that it was another piece of cake. There is not that much in that part of the state, or that part of the country for that matter; a lot of trees blanketing a lot of rolling hills. The road took us all the way to within a few dozen feet of the summit. We parked the car, walked the short distance, quickly (and quietly I might add) and took our photos. The sign located at the highpoint was supposed to be the highest point per my guidebook. I saw that a nearby tree was in fact higher than the sign, so I had my photo purposely taken with one foot placed at the base of the tree while the sign was clearly visible behind me.

As Mike took my picture, he said, "I still don't understand why you want your photo taken."

"In case. I told you back at Mount Mitchell."

"Whatever."

After the photo shoot, we got back in the car and finally headed off to my final destination in Atlanta. I gave my dad a call to let him know that I was on my way.

It turned out to be a very good thing that I went to my dad's that day. When we arrived, my dad had me call Anna right away. She had called him while I was up in the mountains and said that she was experiencing the same symptoms I had prior to me coming down with my bout of Meningitis. This thoroughly scared the hell out of me. I immediately gave her a call to let her know that I was now on my way home. My dad booked me the earliest flight, I said my goodbyes to Mike, and then my dad quickly chauffeured me to the airport. I was still in total agony from my knee and got a lot of stares as I ran to my gate like the Elephant Man, but everybody got out of my way and I was in the air within two hours of talking to her.

My flight had a stop in Chicago, and we were placed into a thirty minute holding pattern just before we landed due to heavy snow. As soon as the pilot announced the hold, I heard the music from *Planes, Trains & Automobiles* start playing in the back of my mind. After we finally landed, I found a phone booth and called Anna to see how she was doing. I was still hours from being home and wanted to make sure she was OK. Remarkably, she said that during the time it took me to get from Atlanta to

Chicago that she started feeling much better. What a huge relief this was to me; to both of us. When I finally got home to Anna that night, she looked and sounded great and told me she was feeling so much better since we last talked in Chicago. I was so happy she was OK because I didn't want her to have to go through what I did when I had it. We held each other for a long time that night.

Being home also meant that highpointing was now over for me. Anna was glad to hear this news and I was somewhat relieved to tell her. But as we talked about it, there was something in the back of my mind now making me wonder if I had made the right choice or not. I knew it was the 100% right decision for me to come home to Anna that night, but telling Mike back in Virginia that 'I was done highpointing for good' might had been too rash of a decision. I was now a little confused on the issue. I had already put so much of my time and effort into this grand endeavor. Maybe I had jumped the gun here a little. Regardless, it was awesome to be home with my kids and in the arms of my beautiful wife.

Mike did continue on with the trip as planned after we split ways, and completed the summits of Georgia, Tennessee, Florida, Alabama, Mississippi, Louisiana and Arkansas. I was glad to hear that he had in fact completed them all. Strangely enough though, I did feel a little bit of jealousy. I wished things had turned out differently during that hike in Virginia and was able to complete all of the mountains with Mike. I had to keep telling myself that it really didn't matter because I still would have flown home to be with Anna regardless.

It was about a year later when I finally realized what was going on between Mike and me during those final two days. Basically, we had been planning this trip for a very long time, Mike postponed the trip when I was ill to allow me to heal, and I ended up quitting right in the middle of it all anyway. We had done all those previous trips together, as well as the numerous trips and highpoints we planned on doing together in the future to accomplish the goal we set for ourselves. This all came crashing down because of my hasty decision, and I totally understood why Mike felt the way he did.

I didn't keep in contact with him for months after this trip. He had quit our company in December 1993 (a little over a year before this trip), and he hired back in June 1995 (a few months after this trip). I heard through the grapevine that he was planning on participating in the 100th running of the Boston Marathon in 1996, and to top it off he was planning on completing all the highpoints of New England as well. I didn't realize that he was still chasing *our* goal. I hadn't even thought of highpoints since the night I got home from Georgia. I had totally blown them off up to this point, but this got me thinking about them again. I thought about it for a few days, and re-assessed my thoughts on the whole idea, as well as on our friendship. I approached him on the idea that I go with him. He was both surprised and skeptical on the idea. We talked in depth about our last trip, about the feelings I went through about highpointing, about the way we treated each other, and we came to an understanding. Everything was fine again. That's how friends are supposed to be. I was re-motivated, and ready to go. I couldn't believe I went from not ever wanting to do another highpoint again in my life, to wanting to do a bunch more not even a year later. Some would call that kind of thinking idiotic. I call it… idiotic.

That evening, I started researching the nine peaks in New England for the upcoming trip. It turned out that a couple of them were closed during the time frame we wanted to go, and a few of them were open, but completely covered in snow with very limited access. I called Mike with the information and we ended up canceling the entire trip including the marathon. We placed it on the backburner for a future adventure. I also called Anna to share with her my decision to start mountain climbing again. I forgot her exact response, but it was something along the lines of, "Are you frigging nuts?" Like the good wife she always was, she told me to seriously think about it before making any final decisions; which I did do. It had been a year since my last highpoint in South Carolina, things were good again between Mike and I, and most importantly I had been bit by the highpointing bug once again. Even though the New England trip was canceled, I couldn't wait for an opportunity to get restarted.

That opportunity arose about a year later…

Chapter 8
- The Midwest Extravagonzo

I was scheduled for a job interview in Denver, and decided to take the opportunity to obtain a few more highpoints in the process. I was planning to get the highpoints of Nebraska, Kansas, and Oklahoma. These would be very simple to obtain, were well within reach of Denver, and would only take a couple of days. I called Mike to let him in on the idea and he signed up immediately. He called me back about an hour later and suggested that we also get New Mexico's highpoint as well. He had already done that highpoint on a previous trip of his, but was willing to do it again for me. I was looking at my map as we talked, and I suggested that we also do Texas since it was so close to New Mexico. He again immediately agreed. This was going to be a great trip, and we were going to get five highpoints in the process.

The next day Mike gave me a call and said that he had been looking at his maps, and suggested that we bag another seven highpoints.

"Seven more? Where?" I asked.

"Iowa, Illinois, Wisconsin, Michigan, Minnesota, North Dakota and South Dakota"

"Are you nuts?"

"Why not?" he replied. "We're going to be in the heartland of America. Why not do all the peaks while we're there?"

This sounded logical to me. I thought about it for about two seconds, and then said, "OK! Let's do it!"

He said, "Great! And since we are going to drive all the way from Texas to Iowa, why don't we also get Louisiana and Arkansas as well?"

"But you already did those."

"I know, but you havn't."

"You would do those ones again? Are you sure?"

"Why not?" he said. "We're going to be in the general area?"

How could I argue with that? Mike had obtained these last two peaks after he dropped me off during our previous trip, but was willing to do these two again for me. Mike was a really awesome friend.

What started out as a two-day, three peak trip was now a nine-day, fourteen peak colossal adventure we aptly code-named, "Exravagonzo." About a month or so before the trip, another coworker by the name of Ron decided to join us on our trip. I warned him on what he was to expect and what we expected of him, and that it wasn't all going to be fun and games. He had heard the stories good and bad, and wanted to be a part of the craziness regardless. Ron had a serious foot injury that shattered his ankle a couple years prior. His parents tried to talk him out of this trip because of his injury, but he really wanted to go. We also tried to talk some sense into him, but he said he was healthy and ready for the adventure. We were glad to have him. I just wonder what he thought about the whole ordeal during his flight home alone just two days into the trip.

Kansas Mount Sunflower
4,039 June 1, 1996

Before we landed in Denver, Mike somehow finagled the Delta Airlines flight attendant into filling my Thermos full of complimentary coffee. She went back and brewed a fresh pot for us as we were descending into Denver. Thank you Mike for having the balls to ask for something like that, and thank you to the flight attendant who had the balls to do it.

We knew we were going to rack up some serious mileage on this trip; I figured about 5600 miles total. Of course we don't disclose that kind of information to the car rental agencies. When we picked the car, the guy at the desk said, "Hey, you guys are in luck. You get a brand new Chevy Lumina with only seven miles on it."

"Seven miles?" Mike asked. "Don't you have anything else with a little more mileage on it?"

"Why?" asked the clerk.

"Umm, uh, in case we have trouble with it; being a new car and all," Mike answered.

The clerk responded, "If you have any problems, just give us a call and we'll take care of it. We service the entire Denver area."

'How about from North Dakota?' I mumbled to myself under my breath. Mike elbowed me in the ribs to shut me up.

As soon as we got in the car, I slapped my new radar detector up on the windshield, poured myself a cup of hot Delta coffee, and we were off. One thing I vividly remember from that night as we were driving east on Interstate 70 away from Denver were the moonbeams. I had never seen a moonbeam before. The moon was so bright, shining through the clouds. It was absolutely beautiful. The beams were almost like spot lights shining on the ground from the heavens above. I've never seen them since.

The excitement began to grow exponentially after we crossed the border into Kansas. Almost as soon as we entered the state, we found ourselves on a gravel road that would lead us for twelve miles to the highpoint. The dirt road we were on was so good that I was actually able to drive seventy miles per hour on it in places; which I was doing when two deer ran out in front of me. We didn't hit them, but it sure put a wet spot on the seat. Mike responded to the situation by saying, "What the hell are deer doing out here in the middle of nowhere? Shouldn't they be in a zoo where they belong?"

We landed in Denver at 9:30PM, and were standing on the Kansas highpoint by 1:00AM. Not too shabby. The highpoint was in the middle of a corn field or something. It was too dark due to cloud cover, so we couldn't see very much. As I parked the car, I turned around to look at Ron and said enthusiastically, "Welcome to your first highpoint; only 47 more to go."

"Wow" he said with a big smile on his face. "How many do you have left?"

"I don't know. Um… this is my 17th, so… 31 more to go."

Mike then said, "Don't you mean 33?"

"Nope! Remember? I'm only doing the lower 48."

Well, I am doing all fifty, and we'll never get to your 18th one if we don't get our photos and get out of here."

With that, we all jumped out of the car and took our photographs. The highpoint owner had created a small shrine on the summit, including a large sculpture of a sunflower fabricated entirely out of railroad spikes all welded together. There was also a mailbox that housed a guest book that we all signed, as well as an open invitation by the land owner for highpointers like ourselves to stop by their home for a visit. Being that it was the middle of the night, and we were on a very tight schedule, we all agreed that this didn't really fit into our plans; not to mention the fact that they probably wouldn't have appreciated our visit at such an ungodly hour. Afterward, Mike then proceeded to give both Ron and me one his new traditional "Highpoint hugs" as he called them.

As Mike and Ron took some time to explore the area around the highpoint, I took a moment to reflect on how absolutely cool this all was. Here I was now in the heartland of America continuing a dream I set for myself so very long ago; a dream that I gave up on just one year prior. I thought about all those times in the past when I had some serious doubts about all of this, and now was questioning myself as to why everything was all of a sudden OK. My thoughts were disrupted when I heard the car doors slam shut. I looked over to the car and saw two eager faces staring back at me. I climbed back behind the wheel, poured myself another cup of still hot Delta coffee, and we all headed off to Oklahoma's panhandle.

Oklahoma Black Mesa
4,973 June 1, 1996

Even though it was a four mile hike to the peak, 99% of the elevation gain took place in $1/8^{th}$ of the distance due to the fact that this peak is located on top of a mesa. We were following what we thought was the trail to the top, but it seemed to be just skirting along the side of the mesa. We were getting a little impatient and knew the highpoint was on top somewhere, so we went straight up the side instead. This is when Ron surprised me by taking two expandable walking sticks out of his backpack and started to use them.

"What's going on there?" I asked him.

"I am just trying to be careful not to reinjure my foot again"

"Are you still having problems with your foot? I thought you said that you were 100% for this trip?"

"I am. I'm just being careful".

That is when I started to notice that his pace had slowed way down, and I could see he was having issues with footing as we made our climb up the side. I felt a little bad that we took him this way, but then again he said he was good to go. I caught up to Mike and told him about my observations. Mike got a little bugged about it and responded with, "Well, he just better keep up. That's all I have to say about it." When we got to the top of

113

the mesa, we had a hard time locating the marker because the top was so vast and flat. We walked and walked, and weren't on any sort of trail at all. We were just hiking cross-country while keeping a keen eye out for snakes. This area is known to be infested with rattlesnakes, so we were constantly on the lookout.

I saw something way out in the distance running away from us. It looked like a chicken. "Mike. I just saw a prairie chicken"

"A prairie chicken? HA HA HA!!!"

"What's so funny?"

"There's no such thing as a prairie chicken."

"Well then what was it? I saw a wild chicken out there"

"You better drink some more water because you are starting to see things."

"Look! There it is! See it? Wait… what is that?"

"That's another one of those damn deer that escaped from the zoo last night. A prairie chicken… HA HA HA!!!"

The deer gave us a long curious look, then turned around and ran away from us. As it disappeared into the distance, it's rear-end looked just like a chicken.

We knew the actual marker was about a mile northwest of a little town called Kenton, so I suggested we walk to the south edge of the mesa to see if we could locate the town down below to get our bearings. We spotted the town out in the distance as soon as we reached the edge and determined that we were pretty much on track. We just kept heading west from there until we found it. When we spotted the highpoint way out on the horizon, I took out my video camera and taped the momentous occasion. Ron had dropped way behind us by now on account of his foot, but finally caught up to us at the summit. He was trying to be very careful not to injure his foot again, but it was pretty tough not to strain it due to the terrain we had to cross. He was also trying the best he could to hide the situation from us, but it was pretty obvious what was going on. Mike and I were starting to get concerned for him at this point, but we kept it to ourselves.

The marker at the top was pretty impressive; the most impressive one I had seen so far, especially for being way out there in the middle of the desert. It was a man-made, nine foot tall pillar made of dark granite. Mike wanted a photo taken of him standing on top of the marker, so I gave him a boost up. The top of the marker had a nice, thick layer of bird crap on it, but Mike climbed up regardless. There was also another fellow highpointer up there as well by the name of Roland, and after this peak, he was heading to New Mexico's Wheeler Peak... the same place we were going next, (or at least that was the plan).

We took our photos, got our highpoint hugs, and then started back to the car. Wouldn't you know it? We found the trail we were supposed to have taken on the way up. This phenomenon seemed to happen to us a lot. About a mile back towards the car I began to notice Ron was experiencing a little more trouble with his foot, and I was really beginning to think that he would not be able to do a few of the hikes yet to come due to their ruggedness and complexity.

This hike took us a little longer than I had planned, which was due to two factors: not being able to find the trail on the way up, and Ron's foot slowing us down. We were to do Wheeler Peak in New Mexico next, but it was already 11:00AM and we were now two hours behind schedule. At this rate, we would be getting off Wheeler around 9:00PM, which was way too late for a mountain of that caliber. And with Ron's foot giving him problems, this would probably tack on a few more hours. We had a pow wow back at the car and decided to blow off Wheeler for another time and head on down into Texas. This was OK because we still had so many more mountains ahead of us on this trip. Wheeler Peak would have been the tallest, most difficult of the trip, but now that it was off the list, everything else would be easy.

We stopped in the little town of Kenton before we left Oklahoma. The store keeper, Allen, realized that we were highpointers, and informed us that he too belonged to the Highpointers Club. He had never climbed a highpoint, not even the one that he could plainly see every day out the front door of his store. The club had made him an honorary member because he was sort of the local focal point for Black Mesa. He said that just about every highpointer that had climbed Black Mesa had come through his store. He had us look ourselves up in back-issues of the club newsletters he had saved, and had us autograph them wherever we were mentioned. It was kind of neat; he treated us like celebrities. He was a very nice guy, and I hope he's still there the next time I come rolling through.

The drive through New Mexico was a long one. I believe it was well over four hundred miles from Kenton to our next peak in Texas. On some roads, you could see for miles in all directions, and at one point we even stopped right in the middle of the highway to switch drivers. Why not? There were no other cars for miles in all directions either. We stopped in the town of Carlsbad that evening for some dinner before we headed down into Texas. That's when I noticed Ron had developed a severe limp. I brought this to Mike's attention out of concern for Ron. All three of us talked about it a little, and decided to go for Texas anyway. Ron was still very motivated at this point and didn't want us worrying about him. The hike in Texas wasn't going to be that difficult anyway, so what could go wrong?

Texas Guadalupe Peak Attempt # 1
8,749 June 1996

We got to the trailhead of Guadalupe Peak about 7:00PM, and were on the trail about an hour later. Before we started, a camper informed us that a couple bobcats were heard earlier in the day right up the trail from us which put us a little on edge. The hike started out a little slow going because of Ron's foot, but that was perfectly all right. We understood. We just wanted to bag this mountain and we had all night to do it. The reason we planned this climb at night was to avoid the fierce Texas heat during the day. To that point, that was the only highpoint we ever 'planned' for a night attack. All the others (with the exception to Mount Hood) just happened to end up that way.

About thirty minutes into the hike, we heard some crunching noises coming out of the brush down the hill from us. Something was walking around out there in the dark.

"What is that?" I asked in an obviously nervous voice, "Is it a bobcat?"

We all stood perfectly still while shining our flashlights out into the darkness. It was so quiet. All you could hear was our breathing and the crunching coming out of the brush. Whatever it was, it was walking real slow, one step after another, like it was stalking us. Ron slowly turned his flashlight out towards the source of the noise. There, looking back at us was a pair of spooky, yellow glowing eyes. A chill went right up my spine.

"What the hell is that?" Ron whispered in a semi-frightened tone as we all huddled a little closer together.

We just stood there frozen, staring into those deadly eyes staring right back at us. It wasn't making any moves, and either were we for that matter. Whatever it was, we didn't want to startle it into attacking us. Then all of a sudden it bounced away into the darkness. It was a damn deer! Then Mike said with a huge smile on his face, "What are deer doing out here in the middle of nowhere? Shouldn't they be in a zoo where they belong?"

We all laughed, but then he said in a more serious tone, "You know, I don't care what it was. Let's walk closely together... single file. A bobcat won't attack anything with six legs"

"Really Mike? Where did you learn that golden tidbit of information?" I asked. I laugh every time I think of that, but you know what? He was probably right.

We got to a point on the trail that we later dubbed 'Bat Alley'. It was a real dark part of the trail shrouded in trees on the North side of the mountain. As we were walking, something flew right by my head a couple times.

"Mike!" I exclaimed, "Something keeps buzzing by my head!" It happened again as I was saying it. I looked up the trail to see if Mike had heard me, and he too was waving his hands and arms up in the air like I was doing.

"I know! It's funny you should say that! I think it's a bunch of bats!" he shouted back. Sure enough, bats were buzzing us, probably eating all the insects we were disturbing as we were walking up the trail. They weren't doing us any harm, so I just tried ignoring them which was a little hard to do. Just then Ron stepped on his bad foot incorrectly and screamed out in pain. I went back to him to make sure he was OK. He said he was and to again stop worrying about him.

We were about three miles up the trail at this point when some weird weather had started brewing. Clouds were rolling in very fast and things just didn't seem right. We got together to figure out what we were going to do. Ron said that he didn't think he could make it the rest of the way to the peak and suggested that he start making his way back down to the car while Mike and I went for the peak. This way we could catch back up to Ron on the way back to the car. Mike agreed with this, but I did not. What if something should happen to Ron on his way back down? Being by himself out here in his condition would not be a good thing. As we argued about it, the weather continued to deteriorate as did Ron's foot. He was in total agony now, so we figured it was in our best interest to get off the mountain and try it again some other day. I felt good over the decision to leave, but felt bad at the same time because we were so friggin close. As much as I really enjoyed having Ron with us, he was seriously starting to hold us back. We had now missed two opportunities and still had so much farther to go. We all needed to talk and talk soon, but not right then. Our main focus was to get off that mountain.

We had a hell of a time getting as far up the mountain as we did, and had it twice as bad getting back down to the car. What should have taken an hour to get down took four. Ron was in excruciating pain, and we were walking at a snail's pace. I was so tired at one point that I kept falling asleep while I was walking. That has never happened to me before or since. It was very bizarre and frustrating. We finally made it back to the car around 5:00AM, and were physically exhausted. Nobody was in the mood to drive, so we decided to snooze for a while. We all drifted off to sleep and were awakened by the car rapidly heating-up as soon as the sun rose. I was behind the wheel, so I started the car, turned on the A/C, and took off east towards Louisiana as Mike and Ron slept.

Ron was so wasted that he slept the entire 550 miles from Guadalupe Peak to Dallas. As we were driving through Dallas on Interstate 20, Ron woke up, looked out the window and saw a road sign stating that the Dallas International Airport was located off the next exit. He told us to take him to the airport, and without any hesitation Mike cut across all the lanes on the freeway to make it happen. When we got him to the departure area, he got out of the car with just the clothes on his back and his two walking sticks. It was a sad sight seeing him limping into the airport terminal.

It was too bad that it turned out that way for him, but I knew what he was going through from my experiences on Mount Hood and Mount Rogers. I also knew it was for the best. I talked to Ron sometime after the trip, and he told me that he still wanted to do highpoints. Not only that, he told me he had the same feeling towards Guadalupe as I did towards Mount Hood. We both wanted to do them again, and kick some butt this time. I did invite him on some other trips, but he was always too busy with other things. He ended up a casualty of a company downsizing and I never heard from him again.

Facing a 250 mile drive to our next peak in Louisiana, I took the opportunity to take a nap before we got there. With Ron now out of the picture, our hikes could now continue as planned without any further delay. I wondered what new and exciting adventures awaited us.

Louisiana Driskill Mountain
535' June 3, 1996

Out of all the highpoints I climbed during my travels, this mountain was by far the spookiest of them all. It was how you felt the first time you rode Pirates of the Caribbean at Disneyland as a small child. Firstly, it was another one of those pitch-black, moonless nights we always seemed to do these hikes on. We were out in the middle of Louisiana someplace, so remote that we didn't see another car or any people for miles. We parked next to an old, run-down church, and then had to walk alongside an old graveyard shrouded in thick ground fog. All we could see of the cemetery were the gravestones peaking out the top of the fog. It had just rained and water was dripping from the mossy trees above us. It was also so quiet that all you could hear were our footsteps, our breathing, and the water droplets as they continually hit the ground. The dogs that were howling out in the distance helped to set the intimidating mood even that much more.

I felt spider webs stretch across my face as I walked through the blackness. This was all very chilling to me. It was right out of a horror movie. I was waiting for the banjo music to start faintly playing out in the woods. I thought I kept hearing things in the trees and kept shining my flashlight on them to see what they were. The noises always stopped every time I did this.

"Will you knock it off!?" Mike said. "You're not going to start that Maryland crap again are you?"

"Maryland?" I replied. "That was fear for your life scary. This is just plain spooky! Do you have chills and goose bumps? I do!"

We got to a gate that was chained shut, but there was an opening just wide enough for us pass through. Spiders had built a solid, thick wall of web across the whole opening. Mike brushed it all away with a stick so we could pass through. Beyond that, there were trails and roads leading in all directions. We kept taking the wrong ones as we searched for the peak, and even walked right over the summit at one point.

After walking downhill for a distance, I finally stopped and pulled out my guidebook for directions. As I pulled it out of its protective Ziploc bag, Mike said, "Hey John! What's that bag for? To keep your book dry? HA HA HA!"

"You still remember that?" I said with a huge smile.

"How's it goin' eh!? And I will keep reminding you of it forever."

"I know you will. That's becoming quite obvious."

Mike shined his flashlight onto my book so we could study it. The light was so intense in the total blackness that it made my eyes want to explode. I could barely make out the writing because it was so blindingly bright. When we were done with the book and Mike had turned his flashlight off, the total opposite occurred and we had to wait for our eyes to adjust back to total darkness again. We figured that we were going down the back side of the mountain and had passed the highpoint somewhere. Not only was this such a familiar theme during my highpointing journeys, but it was also really funny to me this time because Mike had been there just one year prior and should have known basically where it was we were going. We went back up the same way we had just came down and almost tripped on the very small sign marking the highpoint. We had walked right by it the first time, and if it *were* a snake, it would have definitely bit us.

To date this was the lowest highpoint I had ever accomplished; standing at a staggering 535 feet above sea level. I have been asked on several occasions why I even bother with the short ones, or that it all seems, "So silly," or, "Such a waste" to go all that way for nothing. My answer is always, "It's not nothing. It's my dream. It's my goal to stand on top of the highest point of every state in America. Short or tall, I need to do them all. There is no exception." They never seem to get it, but that's totally OK because they don't need too.

I also took a little time at the top to think about Ron and how he most certainly would have had no problems getting up there. Mike felt that same way and wished he could have done this one with us. But what lied ahead of us on some other peaks would have posed some serious issues. It was a sweet and sour kind of feeling. I wished he was there, but I was glad he wasn't. We knew he was most likely home by then, with his foot elevated drinking an ice-cold beer and that was a good thing.

Mike, always trying to keep to the schedule, told me to get my book out so he could take my photo and we could get going. I had forgotten how powerful a flash was in pitch darkness when he took my photo. I was very surprised my eyeballs didn't detonate. As I put my book and flag back into the Ziploc, Mike said, "Hey John! What's that bag for? To keep your book dry? HA HA HA!" I don't think that one will ever get old. On the way back down to the car, we had to go through the small opening in the gate again. Those spiders had apparently got very pissed-off at what we did to them earlier, and had almost completely rebuilt their web fortress in the thirty minutes since we tore it down the first time.

It was now off to Arkansas. Not your Kansas, or my Kansas... Ar-kansas. (Another Mike-ism). It was about 2:00AM, and my turn to drive. I was feeling a little drowsy, so I took a Vivrin chased by a big mug of hot coffee that Mike had obtained for free somewhere along the line. After about fifteen minutes of driving I was more than wide awake. Mike asked me if I wanted him to drive.

"Nope! I'm good for another two hundred miles!

Arkansas Signal Hill
2,753' June 3, 1996

Getting to this peak was one of the slowest parts of our odyssey. Driving the two hundred miles of small, back-country roads in Louisiana and Arkansas was painful. I also learned that when driving through those small southern towns in the middle of the night to obey all speed limits. My radar detector went off in every town. I reset the cruise control to match every posted speed limit for the entire trip to Signal Hill.

My radar detector measures four strengths of radar, and a light bar illuminates showing the strength. When it lights up one notch, it means there is radar in the area, but it's usually just a warning and we don't pay it too much attention. It's actually kind of an annoyance. When it lights up two notches, it usually means we are coming up on an area where a cop has radar on, but it's not beaming in our general direction. In this case we keep our eyes open, but still don't pay it too much mind. Three notches means somebody right by us, and I mean right by us, is being hit by radar, but we're not. We do slow down for this one because it could be us next; and sometimes it is us next. That's when the fourth notch lights up. The radar detector also has an audible alarm doing the same as the lights: A short beep for one notch all the way up to a continuous "beeeeeeeeeeeeeeeeeeeeep" for the fourth.

Driving through these towns was a little ridiculous at times. We would be driving through a settlement, then all of a sudden with no warning, all four lights would illuminate and the alarm would sound at full force. Sure enough there would be a cop hiding behind a church, or down a street behind a tree or a billboard or something. They would just park there all night long hitting every car with radar that passed, patiently waiting for their prey. We were probably the only car that came rolling through some of those towns that night. Every time radar was detected, I played the game of, "Find the cop." I found them every time.

At one point along the way, we stopped to gas up, get coffee, and switch positions. It was about 6:00AM and Mike went into a Subway that just happened to be open. He came out a few minutes later with a huge smile on his face holding his cup of coffee high up in the air.

"Free coffee again?" I asked.

"How's it goin' eh!?"

We finally got to the highpoint around 7:00AM. It had just rained and the air smelled so very fresh and clean up there. It was a very peaceful and quiet place with an occasional bird chirp to break the deafening silence. It was the kind of quiet where all you could hear is yourself walking and breathing, like what we experienced in Louisiana. It was a very short hike to the top where we found a signpost as well as the register. In my guidebook, this highpoint is called Magazine Mountain, but the sign posted at the top stated, "Signal Hill, highest point in Arkansas." So in my eyes, that's what it was: "Signal Hill."

Mike was there a year earlier, and said that the sign did say Magazine Mountain when he was there last. We signed the register, took our photos, jumped back in the car and headed off towards Iowa. As we were driving away from the mountain, Mike asked, "You want to know how Magazine Mountain initially got its name?"

"Sure," I responded enthusiastically.

"Well, when the very first hikers reached the top of Arkansas' highest mountain, they found a vendor up top selling magazines. The hikers asked the vendor if the mountain had a name. The vendor picked up a journal, waved it in the air, and proclaimed 'Magazine!' And that is how it got its name."

Mike looked over at me with his wide-eyed grin as I shook my head in astonishment. Don't worry. There is more where that came from. I promise.

Iowa Sterler Farm
1,670' June 3, 1996

The drive from Signal Hill to Iowa's highpoint was 677 miles of some of the most boring, lonely countryside I had ever had the displeasure of travelling through. This was the second longest stretch of driving we had to do on this trip, and it seemed like the longest. It was especially brutal because most of it was roads and state highways. There were no Interstates anywhere close enough for us to even consider taking.

As we neared this massive behemoth of a mountain, we went through a five mile stretch of road where we were blasted by radar on four separate occasions by four different cops. As soon as the radar detector hit three, it would go to four almost immediately! We were fully conditioned by this time on how to recognize the three strength lights and alarms, and how to get to the correct speed in one heck of a hurry before the fourth light and alarm would sound. In this particular case, we got hit by radar and slowed the car down. When it passed, we got back up to speed, and then get hit by radar again. We quickly got down to the correct speed, then cruised back up and BAM! Slowed down then back up and BAM! It was absolutely crazy.

The Iowa highpoint was unnamed when I visited, but I called it, "Sterler Farm" since 'Sterler' was the name of the family that owned the farm where the highpoint resided. The peak was located on private property and the owner didn't like people out on his land after dark, so we planned it out to where we would get there about midnight and finally get our first real sleep of the trip; it would of course be in the car again, but this was now the norm for us. We would then awaken at 6:00AM, get the peak, then continue on. But we were making killer time and got to the peak at 9:00PM. This would now allow us to continue on through the night to our next stop in Illinois, thus shaving several hours off our trip that we would have spent sleeping.

We parked in the driveway of the owner's house and knocked on his door to ask for permission to access his property. Nobody answered, so we pushed our way through some cows about four hundred feet or so to the designated highpoint. It was at the end of a cattle feed trough. Hanging from the roof was an Iowa license plate that read "HIGH PT", and below that was a small metal box full of key rings in the shape of the state of Iowa with the highpoint information printed on them. Mike and I took one each and threw a bunch of our loose change into the box as a donation.

Although it was very dark and I couldn't see much of anything except for where we were standing, I assumed that the highpoint looked much like most of the country we had just driven through to get there; that part of the country is flatter than flat can be. We took some photos, pushed our way through the cows back to the car, and then we were off to Illinois. Since my visit, the land was turned into a tourist destination and finally given the name of Hawkeye Point.

On the way to Illinois, we had to cross into Minnesota so we could catch Interstate 90 east. Just before we got on the Interstate, we stopped at a McDonalds's for a quick meal and a coffee refill for our Thermos. We were looking for a Subway of course, but had no such luck. After dinner, Mike called a real estate client of his from inside the restaurant. He was trying to close a deal on a house back in California. I went out to the car to wait for him while he was on the phone. Our car was the only car parked outside, and this McDonald's was located right in the middle of a large shopping center's parking lot. We were literally out in the middle of nowhere yet again. That was when a bunch of teenagers entered the parking lot in about ten to fifteen cars and started doing what teenagers do; horsing around and having a good time. They kept driving from one end of the shopping center all the way down to the other in single-file formation. I surmised that there must not be much to do in southern Minnesota on a school night. They drove real slow right past me at one point; one by one, as everybody in each car looked curiously at me. After about six cars or so, I was starting to get a little annoyed and uncomfortable. Finally the last car approached and it stopped right in front of me. It just happened to be the local sheriff, and I guess he did this to block my escape. He flooded my car with light, got out, and walked over to my open window. His partner also got out of the car with her hand resting on her service revolver. I looked up at the cop who was looking down at me, and he proceeded to ask me a question in a way that only a cop could ask it: You know the way, with that slow, sarcastic tone that only their kind can speak: "Why are you here and what are you doing?"

"Are you seriously asking *me* that question?" I responded.

He stood there and stared at me waiting for me to answer his question. I looked at the female officer who started walking around to the passenger side of my car with her hand still resting on her weapon. I looked back at the officer who now had his hand on his as well.

"I just had dinner here and I am waiting for my buddy to come out so we can get going." I started to get a little annoyed and continued sarcastically, "What's up? Am I doing something wrong here? Is it illegal to sit in a car in front of a McDonald's here in the great state of Minnesota?"

Again with the long silent stare from the cop who was now smirking.

"I don't know what else you want me to say. I was just sitting here when all of those kids you were following passed me. I don't get it. Why are you asking me this? Why aren't you asking them what's going on?"

He gave a sarcastic laugh; they both got back in their squad car, and took off after the others. "What the hell? Did this really just happen?" I asked myself.

When Mike got back to the car, I told him what had just happened, and he immediately responded with, "Well it figures being in Minnesota and all. Hey. Do you know how Minnesota got its name in the first place?"

"No idea. It's probably Native American in origin I'm sure."

"No, it's not. When the first settlers arrived in Minnesota, a man asked 'What is the name of this beautiful land we are in?' Next to him on a boardwalk was a vendor selling different kinds of flavored sodas. Right after he asked his question, a child asked the vendor for a minnie soda. The man exclaimed, 'Minnesota? I love it.' And that is how Minnesota got its name."

I looked over at Mike who was sporting his usual wide-eyed grin and said, "You're killing me with this stuff. Shouldn't you be sleeping or something?"

"How's it goin' eh!?"

It wasn't but a few minutes later when I got us onto Interstate 90 heading east and I looked over at Mike who was already passed out. He is one of those people who can sleep anywhere at any time. I am not one of those people, and I had not had any decent sleep since we started this whole thing back in Denver. We had only been driving about fifteen minutes when all of a sudden I couldn't keep my eyes open any longer. I pulled the car over on the shoulder and woke Mike up. He responded with, "Damn! We're here already?!" After I explained to him that he had only been sleeping about fifteen minutes and that I really needed to get some sleep, he popped a Vivrin in his mouth, chased it with a huge gulp of coffee, and we were off to Illinois.

Illinois Charles Mound
1,235' June 4, 1996

Mike drove all night to the Illinois border while I slept in the backseat of the car. He brought along his sleeping bag that was rated to zero-degrees that he usually used for his high country hiking. Not sure why he brought it on this trip as it was too cold to sleep without it, and too hot to sleep with it. I ended up tossing it aside because it just didn't work. Because I had not had much sleep on this trip, I was pretty miserable back there at first. No car's backseat is comfortable when trying to get some sleep, but I was so tired that it just didn't matter for very long. Just inside of Illinois as the sun was starting to rise, Mike had finally had enough and really needed some sleep as well. He awakened me from my unpleasant slumber and I woke up covered in sweat because I had somehow covered myself in his damn sleeping bag during the night. I changed my clothes, poured myself a cup of stale, lukewarm coffee, and had us back on the road in no time. Boy I needed that sleep. I slept all the way through Iowa without waking once. Mike was just getting settled in the back of the car when I asked, "So, what did Iowa look like anyway; since I slept through the whole damn state?"

"Corn."

Because our next peak was only about an hour away, Mike wasn't going to get much sleep; but Mike being Mike, was out within minutes. We crossed the Mississippi River yet again, and followed several narrow country roads through a lot of rolling hills and farmland to get to the highpoint.. There was a light mist over the landscape, and the way the rising sun hit it made it unbelievably tranquil and beautiful. I was so appreciating the fact that I was seeing this because I never got to witness anything like this back home. I found our turn-off and followed the picturesque dirt road about a half mile through the woods to a gate where we needed to park. We would have to walk the final short distance. After I parked and turned off the motor, I looked back at Mike and said gently, "Mike. We're here"

He awoke suddenly and said, "What?! Wait. We're already here? How can that be? We just switched places a couple of minutes ago."

"Um, I don't think so. You have been back there snoozing away for a good hour. Come on. Let's get this peak, and then you can get back there for more sleep on the way up to Wisconsin."

"Sounds good to me. Let's go."

Charles Mound was very beautiful and very green. It was early morning when we arrived and everything really seemed crisp and quiet. It was a very peaceful place and the only thing that broke the silence besides our footsteps were the chirping birds. We walked the small distance to the peak, took our pictures, got back down to the car, and we were off to Wisconsin.

As one can probably tell by now we don't spend much time on the peaks. Our goal is to stand on top of them, take some pictures, and that's about it. People have also asked me, "Why don't you stay longer?" Well, to answer quite frankly... "Why?" I accomplished my goal, why stay? It does seem funny to drive hundreds of miles to a place that we stay for only a few minutes, but that's the way it is. We accomplished what we set out to do. Some peaks are worth a longer stay like Mount Whitney, but not too many others.

Wisconsin Timms Hill
1,951' June 4, 1996

On the way from Illinois to Wisconsin, I started to wonder about all of my distant family I had scattered between the two states. I had family spread from Chicago, half way up into Wisconsin. When I visited as a young teen back in 1975, there were cousins everywhere. I knew that by now those cousins must have had even more cousins, and that my family must be huge by now; Irish Catholics. My mom was always close to them and always stayed in touch. Me? Because I really didn't know them except for my one visit, I let her take care of all the family stuff. Maybe someday in the future I would reach out and make a connection; there would be no time on this trip that was for sure.

As I was driving north, I was beginning to realize that Wisconsin was a very pretty state, and so green. The area around the peak was just beautiful. The whole state seemed very green, very clean, very un-crowded, and so... green. The road leading to this peak was dirt and it gently rolled through the forest covered hills to the park where the summit was. The forests up there are birch and elm, and the roads were covered by their amber leaves.

There were two towers at the top, one wooden (for visitors), and the other was made of steel which was some type of look-out, radio tower or something. We climbed the wooden one to the top to take our photos and to take in the beautiful vistas. When we got off the tower, Mike decided to climb the metal tower as well. I did not climb it, but he said that his hands were frozen by the time he got to the top. There wasn't much more to do there, so when he got down off the tower it was off to Michigan.

Michigan Mount Arvon
1,979' June 4, 1996

We needed to get Michigan's peak before the sun set because the trail system up there was known to be very confusing; especially at night. We were very pressed for time at this point. We had shaved off several hours the day before in Iowa, but reassessed our itinerary after Timms Hill and made a new schedule. If we were going to stay on this new timetable, we needed to get the mountain that evening. We stopped on the Wisconsin / Michigan border in the tiny hamlet of Land O'Lakes to check the car's motor oil and discovered that it was down a quart. We burned a quart of oil in a brand new car. Don't ever buy a rental car. You might end up with one that Mike and I had on one of our trips.

As we were driving along the south shore of Lake Superior on our way to Mount Arvon, we came to a stretch of road through a forest of cottonwoods. They were all shedding at once and it looked as if it was snowing. It was all over the road. As we drove through it, it all got flung up in the air behind us. It was pretty cool.

It had just rained before we got to the peak, so the dirt roads we had to take to the trail were pretty muddy. There was one spot on the road that was washed out with a two foot wide by one foot deep crack running across one side. Somebody had rolled a huge boulder into the crack so cars could cross it. As Mike approached it, I thought he would take it easy as he crossed it. Instead, he gunned it and missed the rock; "BAM!" Boy we hit that thing hard. It was a good thing we didn't screw up the alignment or blow out a tire. We still had about two thousand miles to go. Oh well. Not our car.

We found the trail, and hiked to the top. The book was right about it being a somewhat confusing trail system. It was just a bunch of old logging roads that criss-crossed everywhere. We just followed the instructions as they were spelled out in the book and we found the peak with no problems at all. There were many stream crossings and the trail was very muddy. The sun was setting rapidly, but we made it up and back to the car with a little light to spare. There was this one spot on the trail where a hollow log was buried under the road so water could flow through.

It was while we were taking photos on the summit that I realized that this peak was also a huge milestone for me. It was my halfway point. I now had 24 peaks completed with 24 more to go! I really couldn't believe that I was halfway there. I was over the hump. I excitedly told Mike who then realized that he too had crossed that milestone a few peaks back in Iowa. We gave each other our traditional highpoint hugs, and then started heading back down to the car before it got too dark. During the hike back down, I started thinking back to when I was sitting on Humphreys Peak almost exactly five years prior rejoicing in my triumph of my very first highpoint. I remember thinking to myself how hard this was all going to be and how long it was sure to take. Well, here I was only five short years later, and already half way to my goal. Would it take only five more years to get the other 24? I asked Mike for his opinion and he said that it was definitely a possibility and that we should try and plan it out that way. I fully agreed.

We made it back to the car and were now off to Minnesota. When we arrived back to that large crack with the rock in it, I insisted that Mike let me guide him across it this time which we did with success. We passed another car on its way up to the peak. We knew it had to be another highpointer due to the fact that he was reading the same highpoint guidebook as we had while he was driving. He flagged us to stop and asked for directions and conditions. We gave him easy instructions and told him to get going before it got too dark. I sure hope he made it all right.

Minnesota Eagle Mountain
2,301' June 5, 1996

We had to stop for gas somewhere in Wisconsin, and it was now my turn to drive. Mike had to shake me awake from my deep slumber, and I slowly crawled over to the driver side of the car as he pumped the gas. I pulled out of the station as soon as he got back in the car. I asked him which way I should turn out of the driveway, but he was already fast asleep in the time it took me to drive the fifty or so feet from the pump to the driveway. I made a right hand turn onto the highway and unfolded our map to see if I was going in the right direction. When I looked up from the map, I was headed straight for a curb. "Whoa!" I shouted as I quickly swerved to avoid going up on a sidewalk. Mike smacked his head on the passenger window and never woke up. He just gave a snort and that was it.

I had made the right decision making that right-hand turn, and drove all night up the west side of Lake Superior almost to the Canadian border. I had not relieved myself since back in Michigan some eight hours earlier, so I gently pulled off the road to answer the call of nature. I left the car running and quietly got out and closed the door. Mike shouted something to me as I was walking around the back of the car. I went back and opened the door to see what he said while giving my, 'I gotta go' dance.

"What?" I asked.

"What are you doing? Get the car off the road!"

"What?" as I gave him a look like he was crazy.

"Get the car off the road!"

"What are you talking about? I'm not on the road!"

He was back asleep before I even finished my sentence.

I closed the door and went back behind the car again to take care of business, got back in the car and found the actual trailhead about ten minutes later. Mike woke up for real this time and couldn't believe we were already there. He slept the entire way. We decided to get a couple hours shut-eye until 6:00AM when we would start our hike. I set my alarm for 5:45 and went to sleep.

I was awakened by the sun and said, "Boy the sun sure is bright up here this early in the morning." I was saying this as I looked at my watch. "Hey! Mike wake up! It's 7:00! Were late! We got to get going!" Mike said he had heard my alarm go off earlier, but thought I was still setting it. I must have turned it off in my sleep.

This was a nice hike, but the trail was very rocky. We had to walk on boulders for the entire distance. This was a very unpopulated, remote part of the country again. About half way up to the top, the mosquitoes started practicing their tactical maneuvers on us. There were thousands of them. Mike pulled out his trusty REI Bug Juice and we had no more problems. They were huge though. After we covered ourselves with the repellant, they would fly right into me, and deflect off.

The scenery was awesome and the trail took us right by a beautiful lake that I just had to stop and look at for a while. Living in Los Angeles County, there are no natural lakes to be found anywhere, and I am always amazed at their tranquility and beauty.

Wearing my highpointers tee-shirt
Mike awarded me back on our Colorado Climb

The elevation gain for this trail is six hundred feet, but 99% of this gain was in the last 1/4 mile or so. The sign at the top said that Ulysses S. Grant's son's cousin's roommate's brother-in-law was the first to climb the peak (or something like that). I took out my camera to take some photos, and a huge mosquito tried to steal it. I'm telling you, these things were big! I told Mike I was now over the hump and going down the other side with highpoint number 25 completed. He laughed and bragged that he was still a couple ahead of me. On the way back down the mountain, my knee started giving me problems again, but I dealt with it the best I could and got myself back to the car at a very slow pace. This was the very first time my knee gave me any problems since my hike in Virginia. I thought it was interesting that it was only giving me problems when I hiked. Again I surmised that it was due to sitting in a cramped car for hours on end, then pushing them to their limits climbing these mountains. It looked like I needed to start paying closer attention to this and maybe do some stretches before all my future hikes; it never happened.

It was time to start our seven hundred mile stretch from Eagle Mountain to White Butte, North Dakota. The one thing I noticed while driving through Minnesota was that there were lakes everywhere. I am guessing there must have been at least 10,000 lakes in that state. As we were driving, Mike tried counting them all, but he ran out of fingers, toes, legs, arms, etc. He counted up to about 9,999 lakes, and simply gave up; there were just too many to count. All of that aquatic mathematical activity got us hungry, and because it was so close to lunch time, we looked for and easily found another Subway to visit in Duluth. After that, it was time for another Mississippi River crossing in St. Cloud, and then Interstate 94 west through North Dakota for the next six hours.

As we were nearing the Minnesota / North Dakota border, we were surrounded by three tornado watches. Out in the distance from every angle, you could see where huge areas of the countryside were just being pounded by rain and hail. The news said there were reports of golf ball sized hail and tornados actually touching down. Not being used to this kind of weather, I was understandably a little nervous and concerned for our well being, but as soon as we crossed into North Dakota it was all pretty much behind us. What a ride that was. I wondered if this was some sort of dire warning of things to come. How could it be though? Per the guidebook, North Dakota's highpoint was going to be just like the previous seven peaks: Park the car, walk a short trail, take our photos, then be off to the next mountain. When this next hike was all over, Mike told me that we would look back on that night someday and laugh about it all.

North Dakota White Butte
3,506' June 6, 1996

After driving for twelve hours since we left Eagle Mountain, my excitement began to grow as we finally got off Interstate 94 and headed south towards White Butte. The road we were on took us into the tiny farming community of Amidon, North Dakota. It was about 11:00PM as we rolled into town, and that is where Mike almost passed a parked police car while going seventy miles per hour in a twenty-five mile per hour zone. There appeared to be a cop sitting inside the car and Mike let out an expletive as he slammed on the brakes and slowed the car down to 25 miles per hour within about
1.2 seconds.

"What in the hell are you doing Mike!" I asked as I peeled my face off the windshield.

"A cop!" he nervously shot back.

I looked at the cop car as we slowly passed and started laughing. "That's not a real cop! It's a mannequin! HA HA HA!"

"It's not a mannequin, he's a real cop! Stop staring at him!" he shot back, "You're making it totally obvious that we were speeding!"

"You WERE speeding, but that's not a real cop or cop car. And if it was, how obvious would that had been the way you slowed down so quickly?" I couldn't stop laughing as we passed him. The town had dressed him up in a uniform, some sun glasses, and everything else to make him look as realistic as possible. They had him positioned in the car to where he was looking out the driver's window right at us as we passed. What made it even funnier was that he was wearing sunglasses in the middle of the night. I will never forget that.

It was colder than you could imagine, so I suggested we pull over somewhere in town and get our cold weather gear on before we got to the trail. We pulled into a feed yard and proceeded to change at the car; always within the watchful eyes of our friendly stuffed police officer that I hastily nick-named Bob. Mike asked again, "Are you sure he's not real? He's probably over there wondering what the hell we're doing."

"Yeah. And Bob will come over right when we're half-naked changing our clothes. Will you relax! If he was real, he would be writing you a ticket right now."

"I don't know," Mike said in a disbelieving voice as he continually watched out for Bob.

After we changed, we had to go back to our turnoff while passing our stuffed friend a second time. The trailhead happened to be somebody's driveway to their farm, so we quietly parked in the darkness so they wouldn't see or hear us. As I said before, some people don't take too kindly to strangers on their land after hours. We didn't want to disturb them so late and we didn't want to make ourselves known.

We followed the book's directions towards the peak. It was so dark, we needed flashlights to walk. We could barely see the outline of the Butte way out in the distance, but in the darkness we couldn't tell how far out it was. Per the guidebook, we were to walk up a dirt road to a gate where it would be cross-country straight south from there. We found the gate within minutes.

After we went through the gate, I looked back to the farm house where we were parked and noticed that the house and barn were lit by a single porch light. There was another light about a mile east (to the right) of where we were parked. I told Mike, "On our way back down to the car, the light to the left will be ours," as I pointed them both out to him. He agreed and then we proceeded on towards the peak.

There was no visible trail at all. We were tromping around in the pitch-black darkness trying to find this thing, then all of a sudden we were face to face with a white cliff going straight up. "Hey, this must be White Butte!" Mike said, "And the peak must be up there somewhere." That made perfect sense to me. We literally almost walked right into this thing. It was tough, but we were able to climb straight up to the top. It was like climbing smooth sandstone at a sixty degree angle. We kept losing our footing and sliding back down to the bottom. It was kind of funny and something you would only see in the movies. There were a couple times I could just barely touch the top with my fingertips, and then come sliding all the way back down again. Also try to imagine sliding down a steep hill made of sandpaper, while trying to stop yourself with your fingertips. When we were finally able to reach the top, it was a sharp ridge much like the edge of a knife. We were literally hanging there with our bodies on one side, and our arms dangling down the other. We could not stand on it because it really was as thin as a blade. As we looked up and down the ridge, I asked, "How are we going to find the peak if we can't see it? And if we do find it, how the hell are we going to get to it?" Mike had no response. I was tired of hanging there, so I managed to swing one leg over and sit on the ridge with my legs now dangling on each side. Mike followed suit facing away from me.

The higher parts of the ridge were much steeper, and were very difficult to get too. The only possible way to get any higher in our current situation would be to scoot along the edge on our

149

butts until we found the peak. This idea did not sound very comfortable, and who knew how far we would have to do this? We decided to slide down the other side and walk along the back until we saw something more promising. We got to a point where there was a good pass to cross back to the front side, which we did. We continued along the front of the butte, all the while looking up with our flashlights for a distinguishable highpoint. All we could see were the white, sandy cliffs. My guidebook gave stern warnings of rattlesnakes around the peak, and there had been many sightings through the years; sometimes many sightings by one person on one trip. So here we were wading through waste-high brush, not even being able to see where we were stepping. Not too smart, but we kind of figured, since it was about forty degrees, windy, night time, and a chance of rain, we had no worries about snakes. Luckily, we were right.

We were getting into some pretty deep, thick brush, and decided to turn around and try another angle. We knew the general direction of the peak, but still couldn't see it, or anything else for that matter. As we were doubling back, we somehow got up on to a flat area above the surrounding terrain. "This is it!" Mike shouted, "We must be heading in the right direction now!"

"Why do you say that?"

"Because this area looks well traveled... Wait!... Look!... A trail!"

All of a sudden, a faint trail appeared at our feet, and we excitedly followed it up to a metal fence post sticking up out of the ground at an obvious high point. "This is it! We finally made it!" I shouted. I threw off my backpack and got my camera ready for some pictures. I looked over at Mike who was just standing there staring through the darkness. "What's up?" I asked.

"I think I see a much higher ridge out there in the distance." I could barely see it, but it definitely did look higher.

"Damn it!" I grumbled, "Let's go check it out. We gotta be sure we're at the right one!"

I packed everything back up, threw on my backpack, and we headed off in that direction. We ended up back at that same pass we had crossed from the back side to the front earlier, and actually crisscrossed it this time.

"We were already here earlier!" Mike said as he continued walking and searching, "We're doing a figure-8 around this thing!" He stopped for a moment, looked around, then said, "We need to get back up on the ridge again to get our bearings."

We headed back to the knife ridge that wasn't too far from where we presently were. When we thought we had found the knife ridge, we actually found a ridge that was about 1-2 feet wide this time. We were only within yards of where we had been hanging onto the side a short time earlier, and scooting up here on our butts would have actually been a good idea. We managed to get ourselves back up onto the ridge much like we initially did; with a lot of sliding involved. It was windier than hell up there and it always felt as if I was going to be blown off this thing. It was straight down on both sides, and I am sure there would have been a lot of pain involved if that was to occur. We followed the ridge, and the trail started getting better the further we walked on it. Then all of a sudden we found ourselves standing on the actual peak. There was a small marker there to prove it this time. What a huge relief this was, and what a victory.

I took off my backpack, and took out my camera for a second time. I was about to snap my first photo when I looked out towards the farm house where we were parked. I now noticed that there were three lights out in the distance instead of two, and all three of them were about a mile spaced.

"Boy, it's a good thing I took note of those lights back at the gate. Just remember that the light on the left is where we parked the car"

Mike looked out at the lights and said, "I guess because we are so much higher now. We can now see the third light that we couldn't see when we were down by the gate. Yep, I agree. We need to head to the light on the left when we leave."

We took our pictures, waited for the temporary blindness to end, and then started to pack up. It was just as I was putting my guidebook back in the Ziploc bag when I felt the first drop of rain.

"Mike, did you feel that?"

"Feel what?" he said just as it started to rain rather steadily. It wasn't too hard, but enough to get us pretty wet. He then started laughing and said, "Hey John! Why do you keep your book in a Ziploc bag? HA HA HA!!!"

"Exactly! We better get going. It's a couple miles back to the car".

We took off down the mountain, always keeping the light on the left within our view. This sandstone type mountain was really made out of some type of clay that became very slippery when wet. We were slip-sliding all over the place, and our clothes were getting caked in white mud. We made it back to the gate we had passed through earlier, and now only had about a mile left to go to our warm, dry car. We were getting pretty soaked, and all I had on was my typical blue sweat jacket.

Mike was looking over the post that the gate was latched too with kind of a puzzled look on his face, and then said. "This isn't the gate we came through on the way up"

"What?"

"This isn't the same gate. The post on the one we came through was round, not square like this one"

"What are you talking about?" I said, "You noticed that the post was round?! Are you serious? Look. There's the light at the farm house we need to get too. We're going the right way. Let's get going." Mike agreed and we headed off towards the light like a couple of wandering moths in the night.

We soon came upon a deep, dry ravine. "Where'd this thing come from? We didn't cross this on the way up!" I said. Without hesitation, Mike slid down into the ravine and climbed up and out on the other side. I followed suit and found him at the top holding a barbed wire fence open for me to slip through. "And where did this come from?" I asked. I looked out towards our guiding light and said, "Well, I guess we just got a little off track or something. At least our car is right over there waiting for us. Let's go."

Right after climbing through the fence, we somehow ended up walking through a freshly plowed field which was 100% mud. We were sinking in the stuff up to our knees in places. It wasn't too much longer before we came upon another barbed wire fence. Again without hesitation, Mike climbed through first, and then held it open for me to crawl through again. At least the farm house light was still in view which meant that we were going in the right direction. By now we were both carrying about fifteen pounds of mud on each of our boots and legs, which made walking very tough. It was at this point when my friggin' knee started hurting me again. I kept the condition of my knee quiet because I just wanted to get back to the car and not bother Mike with it. We soon came upon a second ravine, this time with muddy water flowing through it. "What the hell is going on here?!" I asked with a little concern in my voice. "There were no ravines or fences on the way up. Something isn't right here."

"Just follow the light," Mike said as we both traversed the muddy ravine.

Then just a few moments later, there was a third fence. We both crossed it this time in total silence. My knee was in excruciating pain to the point to where I was now limping extremely bad. The weight of the mud was just making it worse, and there was nothing I could do about it. We got up to within one hundred feet of the farm house when we both stopped dead in our tracks. "This isn't the right house Mike." I whispered with a lot of concern. The car was nowhere in sight.

"What happened?" asked Mike.

I looked back towards the mountain that was not visible through the darkness and the rain. I then turned and looked back at Mike who was himself looking around in confusion. I then surmised, "Well, the only thing I can guess is that when we were at the top and noticed the third light; we both assumed that it had appeared out in the east, to the right. When in reality, the third light was out to the left. We are at that third light."

"Damn."

"Yeah. Now we need to get to the middle light. That's where our car is parked."

It was about a mile to the east of us through the same muddy plowed fields we just came through, not including all the barbed wire fences and ravines we needed to cross again.

"Well, we have to do it, so let's get going" Mike said.

By this time my knee was absolutely killing me. I finally had to tell him what was going on since I kept asking him to wait up for me. He didn't want to hear any of it because knee or not, we needed to get to the car. We also now had to cross those deep ravines that were quickly filling with flowing water. We slipped into them, sloshed through the water, and struggled up and out the other sides. As we approached the next farm house, I kept having this nightmare that when we got there, it wouldn't be the right one either. My highpointing related anxiety was starting to rear its ugly head again, and I just wanted this nightmare to be over. If that next house wasn't the right one either, I didn't know what we would do. We would probably have to backtrack back to the summit to reestablish our bearings, and I was in no shape to do anything like that. As we walked around the barn at the second house, I told Mike that we could probably seek shelter inside if we needed to; if this wasn't the correct house and all. It was right then when Mike smacked my chest with the back of his hand to get my attention and pointed out our car sitting there hidden in the darkness. What a tremendous relief that was and I felt my anxiety wash away within a second. Even though it was gone, I still hated the fact that I was even dealing with it. Why was I always worrying so much during times like these, or even allowing it to make me a little scared? I was getting tired of it always interfering with what I was doing, but had no idea how to address it. I never talked to Mike or anybody else about it, and I quietly just wished it would go away forever.

We quietly made our way to the car so the land owners wouldn't hear us. It was raining pretty hard now, so hard that we could hardly even hear each other. "What are we going to do with all our muddy clothes and stuff?" I asked. When Ron left us in Dallas, which seemed like eons ago now, he left his ice chest in our possession. Mike suggested that we put all of our muddy gear into the ice chest so we would not get the car dirty. Mike opened the trunk of the car, popped open the lid of the ice chest, and we couldn't believe what we found inside: an empty bottle of peppermint schnapps. Ron must have been self-medicating after Guadalupe Peak on the long drive to Dallas. It was no wonder why he was so quiet the remainder of the trip. Regardless, it was still raining very hard and standing around was doing us no good. We stripped down to our thermal underwear, threw our boots and clothes into the ice chest, jumped into the car, and started our trek to Harney Peak in South Dakota.

It was now about 2:00AM, and our only worry at this point was that we didn't get pulled over for anything since we were both wearing nothing but our thermal underwear. That would have been too funny. I was glad Mike was driving because I was in no condition due to my knee, and I really needed some sleep. I was also looking forward to summiting our final two peaks of the trip the next day; this meant we would be heading on home soon.

During the writing of this chapter, I did a search via Google maps to see if our friendly stuffed officer was still parked in Amadon, ND scaring the hell out of unsuspecting speeders. He is still there and can be found at these coordinates:

Aerial view - 46.482567, -103.321697
Street view - 46.4824432,-103.3195706

South Dakota Harney Peak Attempt # 1
7,242' June 1996

Mike drove from White Butte to Rapid City, South Dakota, and had had enough of driving as soon as the sun began to rise. He pulled into a gas station and woke me out of my deep sleep to ask if I would drive the final leg to Harney Peak. I agreed and proceeded to get out of the car. That's when I realized two things: I was still in my underwear, and I couldn't move my leg without pain shooting throughout my entire lower body. The pain was unbelievable and it hurt no matter how I moved. I needed to get some clothes on before I got out of the car because it was a busy gas station and people were everywhere. This proved to be a huge, painful challenge, but I was able to eventually get it accomplished. I got out of the car and hobbled around to the driver's side leaning on the filthy, dirty car the whole way. Once inside, I told Mike (who was sipping on his recently scored free cup of coffee) about what was going on with me. He made some comment about how the pain was all in my head, and that was the end of that discussion.

When we got to the trailhead I couldn't even get out of the car as the pain was now sharp and excruciating. I told Mike to go up without me, and his immediate response was, "Damn right!" I was in way too much pain to be upset about not being able to hike to the top. I had myself to worry about, and like I have said before on other occasions, the mountain would still be there for another day. Mike put on his running shoes and I watched him run off into the woods. There was no way I was going to deprive him of bagging that peak when we were so close.

Not only was I in agony, but I was also very tired so I decided to get some sleep while he was gone. I moved the car under a tree for some shade, turned off the motor, and I was out for the count. I was only asleep for what seemed to be about a minute when a tap on the window awoke me. It was Mike with those big eyes and huge toothy smile again. I opened the window and asked him what he had forgotten.

"Forgotten?" He answered, "I'm back! Let's get going to Nebraska! Move over, I'll drive."

"What? No really, what did you forget?"

"I'm back. Let me in so we can get going"

"Come-on... you already went all the way to the top and back?

"How's it goin' eh!?"

"Damn! You're an animal!"

I was in such a deep sleep, that the time just flew. It was an eight mile round trip hike, and he ran it in just under three hours. It really did seem like a minute to me. Since I was in the driver's seat and in no mood to move, I decided it was best if I just keep driving. I started the car and headed back down the dirt road the same way we came. Mike told me about his run and how he got lost on the way back to the car, but also that it was still "Awesome." Once we got to the highway, I was going to turn back the same way we came, but Mike stopped me and told me to go the other way. I asked why and he said that there was a crew working on the road about a mile from where we were and there was this cute girl working with them he wanted to see again. "Again?" I asked? "What were you doing on the road a mile from here? Why didn't you come back on the same trail you started on?"

"Because I got lost... remember?" He said with that smile again.

We laughed and went down the road to see 'his' girl. She was still there when we arrived at the work site. She was on my side of the car, so he had me roll down my window to ask her if he could take her picture. She agreed. He took her photo, said goodbye, and we were off. I never asked Mike about the photo, and I had never seen it until it showed up in my company mail a few years later with a note attached. Mike was too much. I do have to say that she was very cute.

We were now off to Nebraska, our last peak on our 14 peak Extravagonzo. After that would be Denver to catch our flight back to LA early the next morning. I did some thinking on the way to Nebraska, and suggested to Mike that we skip Nebraska and get back to Denver as soon as we could to catch an earlier flight home. I still needed to come back to South Dakota someday to do Harney Peak, and could easily do Panorama Point in Nebraska in the process. Mike liked this idea and said he wouldn't mind going on that trip with me even if it meant doing Harney again. "Besides," he said, "I can see my girl again!"

We started making our plans to get to Denver. We were zipping across the states of South Dakota and Nebraska, trying to shave off any time we could to be sure of catching a flight out that night. We had the maps out and were looking for short cuts everywhere. Mike had his calculator figuring where we could shave seconds. We even figured that if we took every corner on the inside, we could save about half of a second each time; actually, that was Mike's thinking, not mine.

We got to an intersection in Nebraska where it was either left or right. Straight ahead was a dirt road that according to the map, would shave off about eight miles. Mike started to ask, "Should we go that w..." Before he could finish his question, I had us going eighty miles per hour down this dirt road through the heart of Nebraska. An 18-wheeler passed us going the opposite direction causing gravel and dirt to fly up everywhere. I couldn't see a thing for a few seconds, but since the road was straight as an arrow, I just kept the car going straight. We were making killer time.

We were just a rocks throw away from the next road we needed to catch, and there was a rail road crossing there with a train coming down the track about 1/4 mile away. If we were just one minute later, we would have been sitting there forever waiting for that coal train to go by. It must have stretched from where we were sitting, all the way back into South Dakota. That sucker was long. If we would have got caught, it probably would have been faster to go back the eight miles to where we started, and go around.

We pulled into a small town which consisted of a couple buildings, a gas station, and a few houses. We decided to stop for gas, and I took the opportunity to call Delta Airlines to make the necessary flight arrangements. I made the call from an old, crusty phone booth while Mike filled the car. The town was so small that the rail road went right through the gas station's driveway. A train just happened to pass through as I was talking to the Delta representative. The phone booth began to shake violently, and the train's Engineer just had to blow the horn as he went by. I could barely hear the Delta guy talking on the phone, but I did hear him laughing. After the train had passed, the guy asked, "Where the hell are you anyway?"

"Believe it or not... I have no idea. I'm in Nebraska somewhere." He laughed.

The Delta representative informed me that it would cost an additional $600.00 each for us to fly home that night. "WHAT?!" I exclaimed over the phone, "When we bought the tickets, they told us that we could take an earlier flight home if we wanted at no additional cost."

The man on the other end apologized and said, "Oh... I'm sorry, it's not $600.00 sir. I made a big mistake".

"You're darn right," I shot back. There was no response, and all I could hear was the clickity-click of him working his magic on the keyboard. He then he said, "Again, I apologize sir. It's only going to be $395.00 each."

"WHAT?! Are you kidding me?!"

He told me there was nothing he could do and that I should get to the airport and work it out there. I slammed down the phone and told Mike what had just happened. Mike's response was, "Just wait 'till we get to the airport. We'll be flying first class on the way home. We'll also get a free airplane out of this too!"

Before we left the gas station, we spread all of our wet, muddy clothes from North Dakota all over the front and rear dashes of the car, and wherever else we could lay them so they would dry out a little. It is hard for me to describe what it smelled like in the car; Interesting is the only word that comes to mind. Later during the drive, Mike crawled into the back seat and packed up all his stuff while I drove the first leg to Denver. We stopped just inside of Colorado to switch places, and took the opportunity to lay out all our wet stuff all over the warm road to dry out a little more. There wasn't anybody around for miles, so why not? We were lucky nobody did drive by though. I have to admit that it would have been a very funny sight to see. After racing across two states to get to Denver in record time, we ended up sitting in bumper-to-bumper traffic the final few miles to the airport.

We returned our rental car with 5502 additional miles on it. I wanted to video tape the guy's reaction when we returned the car with so many extra miles on it, but it was all automated. They just punch in a bunch of numbers into a hand held gizmo, and you're off. When we got to the ticket counter at the airport, Mike was about to let them have it over the additional cost when all of a sudden the man behind the counter said, "No problem sir. Your flight leaves in forty-five minutes from gate 67. Have a nice flight." Mike and I looked at each other and he said, "Cool! Now this is the way it's supposed to be!" Either the Delta rep I talked too didn't know what he was talking about or he fixed it before we got there. In either event, it was all taken care of now and that's all that mattered.

161

We were on the next flight home and Mike ended up sprawled-out across all three center seats of the jet. His head was hanging over into the aisle, and I was just waiting for a flight attendant to push a drink cart into his head or something. Knowing Mike, he would have gotten a free airplane for that one... or just settled for a free cup of coffee. As we landed in Los Angeles, the flight attendant announced the landing, and Mike didn't hear a word of it. He just kept on sleeping. A flight attendant even walked by and accidentally knocked off his fluorescent green hat. She didn't even notice him there. I didn't wake him either because I wanted to see the expression on his face when we landed. "BAM!" The plane landed so hard, I thought we were going to blow some tires. Mike jumped right out of his seats. "What's going on?! Are we home already?!" I thought that was so funny. We caught a taxi to his house, said our goodbyes, and I headed on home. Sitting in evening traffic on Interstate 405 was how I ended my Extravagonzo.

I set out to do 14 peaks on this trip; I did eleven, and Mike did twelve (doing Louisiana and Arkansas for the second time). At that point I had 26 peaks down with 22 to go. What a great trip that was. I couldn't wait for the next adventure. Shortly after our return to the real world, our company adopted a new work schedule to where we got every other Friday off. It turned out that Mike and I were placed on the same schedule. Labor Day was fast approaching, and we both had the Friday before the holiday off. Mike called me and asked what I had planned for my four day week-end.

"I don't know. I don't really have anything planned. Why?" I replied.

"Do you want to go get the ones we missed?"

"The ones we missed? Which ones are those?"

"Texas, New Mexico, South Dakota, and Nebraska."

"Hell yeah!"

162

After I informed the Highpointers Club regarding our Mid-west Extravagonzo, the following appeared in the next issue of their quarterly newsletter: "John White and Mike Gauthier went on a 6 day HPing odyssey covering the entire mid-west from the Rockies to the Mississippi and from Mexico to Canada. The 'Night Shift'. I've read their climbing reports. Have you guys ever thought about climbing in the daylight?"

48 Mountains

Chapter 9
- The Ones We Missed

I was very thrilled and excited to be getting another four peaks. Getting highpoints was always very exciting for me, but getting ones that I had missed for one reason or another made it even more so. Mike only had to get Texas and Nebraska, while I needed all four. This was gearing up to be a great trip for both Mike and I. I just didn't realize at the time that I would be returning home not having completed some of them yet again...

Texas Guadalupe Peak Attempt # 2
8,749 August 30, 1996

I met Mike at his house in Manhattan Beach early in the morning, and we departed on our next adventure together promptly at 4:30AM. Our first stop was to pick up our next rental car. We always used Alamo Rent a Car, and I was now starting to get a little concerned that after all of the miles we had been putting on their cars throughout our adventures that we would someday be denied. By some miracle, they always gave us a car.

There was not much exciting activity driving Interstate 10 all of the way to Texas, but we did arrive at the trailhead at Guadalupe Peak at 7:00PM. It took us 14 hours to drive 1/3 the way across the country, and that to me was not too shabby. We averaged 69.9 miles per hour from His house to El Paso, Texas. (Mike kept very detailed records on this stuff).

During the drive across Arizona, I noticed a couple prisons somewhere between Phoenix and Tucson. There were road signs everywhere stating:

"DO NOT PICK UP HITCHHIKERS"

Standing right below one of those signs was a guy trying to hitch a ride. I wanted so bad to pull over and take a picture of that, but that would be just as dangerous as picking him up. Eventually, I bet somebody was actually stupid enough to do it.

Somewhere near Tucson the song, "What I Like About You" by The Romantics came on the radio. Mike awoke out of his snooze , cranked the volume on full, and sang the whole song at the top of his lungs just as loud as the radio as I sat there watching him in amazement. When the song was over, he lowered the radio back to its original setting and laid back down to go to sleep. I looked over at him with a bewildered look and said, "HellOOOooo! What the hell was that all about?!"

"I LOVE that song!"

"You think?! Holy crap Mike!" He smiled and went back to sleep.

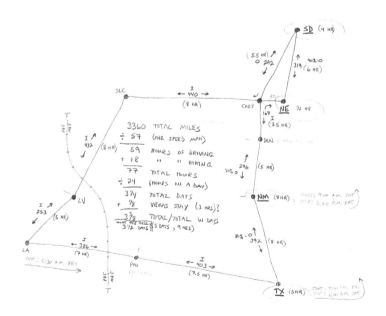

167

48 Mountains

One of my many planning maps.
This particular one was for 'The ones We Missed'

The sky was clear as a bell driving the final distance to the peak. This was good because we planned this trip around the full moon for light. It was going to be full that night, and cloud cover would have defeated the purpose. When we pulled into the parking lot, there was only one available parking spot left, and it was the same spot we had the last time we were there with Ron. As soon as we got out of the car, the clouds started rolling in, and as soon as we hit the trail, the moon was completely gone.

We headed up the trail on a mission to complete this peak successfully this time. There was nothing that could stop us. Mike and I talked a little about our last attempt and how we wished everything would have been different, especially when it came to Ron. But because of the events on that fateful night, here we were again trudging up the same trail just a couple of months later. If Ron would have made it to the top, he most-likely would have completed most of the others on our previous trip as well. But fate threw us a curveball that night, and here we were again.

Because the moon was completely gone, it was very dark and the trail was barely visible. There were these strange tiny bugs; like lightning bugs, that faintly glowed as we passed by them. They were so dimly lit that I had to really concentrate to see them. At our first rest stop, a lone bat buzzed us the entire time we sat there, probably snacking on the lightning bugs we were stirring up. Unlike the last time we were there, this was the only bat on this trip.

It was a very good feeling when we passed the same spot where we turned around the last time with Ron. We paused there for a moment to reflect, and then continued on to the summit. This actually gave us even more motivation to get to the top than we already had. It started getting very foggy at that point, so much so that as we neared the summit, our hair and clothes became totally soaked. Water was dripping out of my hair and down my face. I had to put on my bandanna that I usually use for when I'm sweating. Good thing I brought it. Always be prepared.

We kicked some serious butt to the top. We made it up in two hours, 45 minutes in pitch blackness, and soaking wet! I don't recall if we turned on our flashlights once. We try not to use flashlights on any of our trips unless it's absolutely necessary as this saves precious batteries and bulbs. As soon as we stopped at the top, and took off our packs; we realized it was pretty cold and windy up there. You don't realize how cold it really is until you stop walking. I was shivering, but I didn't want to put my jacket back on because I would have to stop almost immediately after we started our descent to take it back off.

We took our photos through the fog, and headed back down the mountain. We had finally developed a new technique to taking photos at night so that we didn't get punched in the face by the blinding flash: The person taking the photo also shines a flashlight into the face of the other. This worked out well and we ended up using it on all of our following night time climbs. On the way back down the trail, we used our head lamps because of how dark it was. We wanted to see our footing so we wouldn't slip and fall.

About halfway down the mountain, after descending out of the fog, I was stopped dead in my tracks when I spotted up on the trail ahead of me a single glowing eye staring back through the darkness. Mike ran right into me because of how quickly I stopped.

"Why the hell did you stop like that?!"

"Shhhh!"

"What now?!"

"Shhhhh!! Look up there," I whispered. "What the heck is that, and why does it only have one eye?"

"I don't know" Mike whispered back. "Is it a bobcat?"

"I don't know. What do we do? It is sitting right on the trail."

"Get outta here!" Mike shouted. It didn't even flinch.

"I don't think it speaks English Mike." I tossed a couple rocks towards it to make it move, but it just stayed there staring back at us. We started slowly approaching it, but it just stayed there; staring. A bobcat or deer would have moved by now. "Was it a rabbit?" I thought. I wondered if it was in fact a bobcat and what would we do if it charged. I hated this situation so much. As much as I loved to do these hikes, I often felt way out of my comfort zone and very vulnerable during situations like this. As we continued slowly approaching whatever it was, it finally blinked a couple of times and took into flight. It was a huge owl and it flew right over us while making its escape. As small of a situation that was, it was really nerve-racking and made me want to get back to the safety of our car that much quicker.

Just down the trail from Bat Alley, we got to a section that was a little loose due to erosion. I lost my footing, slid, and fell wrong. When I slid, my left leg actually slid out to the left which caused me to spin around and fall flat on my butt. I hurt my butt, hands, and most of all, my left ankle and knee. What was it with my left leg all the time? I sat there for a moment to make sure I was OK to continue. I took it real careful the rest of the way to the car. Everything seemed to be OK, but as soon as we got into the car, my ankle and my knee started in on me... again. I didn't need this. As we were driving to Wheeler Peak, New Mexico, my foot and leg were really starting to hurt. I told Mike that I probably wouldn't be able to do Wheeler Peak because of this. He told me that we still had several hours to go before we got there and to get some rest.

"But I'm the one doing the driving!"

We drove north out of Texas, and continued through New Mexico towards Wheeler Peak. We had to drive that direction to get to our two other planned peaks in South Dakota and Nebraska as well, so we were not going out of the way in case I decided I couldn't do Wheeler. When we got to a certain point in New Mexico, I would have to make the decision on whether or not I would do Wheeler. This decision spot was still two hours away.

As we were driving through New Mexico around 1:00AM, we had to go through one of the most awesome storms I have ever been in. It was unbelievable. Lightning, thunder, and rain so hard that I couldn't see the road. There was lightning on top of lightning. Sometimes it would strike right in front of us with accompanying thunderclap at the same exact moment. When it struck, it blinded us for a few seconds, and the whole car shook like an airplane in bad turbulence. We had to stop the car right on the road at one point because I could not see anything. When we went through Roswell, there were literally rivers crossing the highway that we needed to cross. I was waiting for white water rafters to come floating by it was so bad.

When we got to the Wheeler decision point in New Mexico, I chose South Dakota and Nebraska. My ankle and knee were killing me, and because of this storm, we didn't know if we would be able to do the mountain anyway. Wheeler is notorious for 'mega' lighting storms, and we thought that this would have been one of those times. Leg or no leg, we probably would have blown this one off anyway. When Mike did Wheeler years earlier without me, he got caught in a lightning storm near the top and had to take shelter until it blew over. He didn't like the idea of us climbing it at all this time. We would have been miles away from any kind of help if anything were to happen. Lightning is a very scary and powerful thing. One of my only wishes when it came to mountain climbing was to never come in contact with it. Being over halfway to my goal of 48 mountains, I was having pretty good luck with this one wish so far…

We gassed up in Cheyenne, Wyoming at the intersections of Interstates 25 and 80. When I got out of the car (the first time since New Mexico) my ankle was now swollen and still very painful. I could hardly walk. Harney Peak, South Dakota is an eight mile round tripper. I really didn't think I could do it, and if I did, it would have been very slow and painful. Flashbacks of Ron in Texas kept running through my mind, and I didn't want to go through that. I told Mike we had to skip Harney Peak, and he didn't mind very much since he had done it on our previous trip. I was real bummed out about the situation as I was so close again, but I really had no choice in the matter and I had to look out for myself. Like I said for Harney Peak the last time I was there, the mountain would still be there for another day. So off to Nebraska it was.

Nebraska Panorama Point
5,424 August 31, 1996

When we got to the small dirt road that led to the top of Nebraska, there was a section that was totally covered with mud and a huge puddle the size of a locomotive. Mike asked if we should even proceed. With that, I punched it and plowed right through it. The car went from total white to total brown in a matter of seconds as the mud I flung straight up into the air came raining back down completely covering the entire car in the slimy, brown muck. I couldn't see anything and I didn't want to stop the car to avoid getting stuck in the middle of nowhere. I turned on the wipers so we could see, but it didn't help very much as the mud just got smeared around. I could see just enough that as soon as we passed through the puddle we were face to face with the marker at the top.

It was hard to believe that Panorama Point was over a mile high when I was standing on it. This is another one of those peaks literally out in the middle of nowhere, and the countryside was flat as far as the eye could see. We met a nice family at the top who were locals to the area. They told us that they swung by there once a year to read the register. They were kind of surprised to hear that we had been in Los Angeles just the day before, and had come to Nebraska by way of Texas. They told us about a couple things to see in the area while we were signing the register. They said to see the herd of Bison right across the border in Colorado, and I mean right across the border. The border is a couple hundred feet from the highpoint, and the states are divided by a barbed wire fence. Also about a mile away was the tri-state marker where Colorado, Wyoming and Nebraska all touch at a single point.

We jumped back in the car and had to take the same muddy dirt road away from the peak. I had to even out the mud coverage on the car, right? We went and saw the bison, then drove to the tri-state marker where we enjoyed a scrumptious lunch of Subway Sandwiches while sitting on three states. We got the sandwiches in Cheyenne and had put them on ice for this stupendous occasion. I ate most of my lunch in Wyoming and Nebraska, while Mike stayed put in Colorado.

After all of that craziness, it was time for the long journey home by way of Las Vegas, Nevada. We stopped at the first gas station we came across to clean our headlights because we knew that zero light would have been able to pass through the mud later that night when we needed it most.

Mike enjoying a Subway "on" three states

During that long, lonely drive, I thought a lot about those two peaks I had missed yet again. This was really bothering me to no end. I had traveled all the way to New Mexico and Nebraska twice, only to return empty handed both times. This to me was a stain on my highpointing track record, and I made a promise to myself at that exact moment that there would not be a third failure. I would come back from the next trip to those mountains a victor. I started feeling good again, and the only thing that would complete my morning was an all you can eat pancake breakfast at The Boardwalk hotel and casino for $0.99. Mike was very happy with my choice of restaurants and told me

175

that he was starting to rub off on me a little. After we filled our bellies with too many maple syrup covered flapjacks to count, I found a quarter on the ground, stuck it into a video poker machine, and parlayed it into $10.00 in a matter of two minutes. Things were looking up. When we returned the rental car, the guy who checked the car back in said, "Boy! Looks like we're going to have to run this one through the wash! Where did you guys go to get it so dirty?"

Mike and I both said, "Nebraska!" at the same time.

"What?"

When we got back to work and spread the news to our friends and co-workers regarding our recent undertakings, a small article about us ended up in our Department's monthly newsletter. To this day, I have never figured out who submitted it, but I must admit it was pretty cool and it garnered us a lot of attention:

Did You Know???

That it is John F. White's goal in life is to stand on the highest point of every state in the contiguous 48 United States. He has completed 28 to date including the highest (Mt. Whitney, CA. 14,494'). He has an interesting story for just about every peak he's done so far (and for the ones he's attempted and couldn't do). Ask him about it!!! He has a partner who shares the same goal. His name is Mike Gauthier and also works for Hughes. He got him interested in this madness called "HighPointing."

176

A short time after our trip, I invited Mike to come my house for Christmas. I also told him about my plans to get the highpoints of Florida, Alabama, and Mississippi in March of the following year. These were the peaks that Mike acquired after he dropped me off at my dad's in Atlanta a couple of years prior. I explained how I was going to fly to Atlanta, rent a car, get the highpoints, and then fly back home. You can probably guess what his response was to that:

"You're going in March? Can I go? I know. Let's rent a car from here, drive across the country, bag them, and then drive back home. I bet we can do it in four days! And we can stop in Laughlin on the way home to throw some dice! How's it goin' eh!?" He stood there afterward staring at me with his usual wide-eyed grin, and with that we had our next trip preliminarily scheduled.

Right before the Christmas shutdown at our company, I suggested to Mike that we go for Florida, Alabama and Mississippi during the holiday break instead of waiting until March. His immediate response was, "OK!" Would you have expected any other answer?

Mike showed up at my home to share Christmas with me and my family. Later that evening after dinner, we snuck up to my office to plan out our trip. We dragged out the maps, figured out how many miles between each major city along the way, converted those numbers to time, what times we would be at each city, estimated gasoline costs, etc. We put all this info down on a sheet paper, and we were ready to go. After everybody went home, I asked Anna if I could borrow her car for a few days. I figured why rent a car if I have a perfectly good one at my disposal. After a very long discussion filled with rules about how I was to treat her baby, we were set. I thought it was so cute how much she cared for her car and how serious she was that we do the same. Two days later on December 27, 1996 at 10:56PM, we were on our way to the southeast yet again.

In total, I had visited Panorama Point on three separate occasions:

Climb #1 was for score and was as just told here in Chapter 9.

Climb #2 was with Mike, our friend Joe and myself, and is as told in Chapter 12.

Climb #3 was with Anna, and my two children Zachary and Caitlyn back on June 15, 2003. I secretly planned this highpoint during a family vacation to South Dakota. It was the middle of the night and I was headed east on Interstate 80 through Wyoming. I was getting tired, and everybody else was fast asleep throughout the motor home. I figured it was time for me to pull off somewhere to catch a few winks as well. As I neared the Wyoming / Nebraska state line, I realized that we were only about twelve miles from Panorama Point. This was going to be perfect…

I got off the Interstate and headed south to the Colorado state line. I planned on parking the RV right at the tri-state marker on either Colorado and Wyoming, or Colorado and Nebraska at the same time. It is impossible to park on all three states because there is a large granite marker blocking any attempt. I was good with just two states. The plan was to include waking up in the morning and telling everybody that I slept in Colorado while they slept in either Wyoming or Nebraska. It would be fun.

Now I don't really know where I went wrong, but things almost got really bad. When I crossed into Colorado, I was to take a small dirt road on the left for about ½-mile that would follow the Colorado / Wyoming state line to the marker with Nebraska. I "thought" I found the right road and followed it for almost a mile when the road all of a sudden got very muddy and slippery. Everybody was asleep and I had the RV sliding at angles down the road at times as I struggled to keep it going straight. I knew at that time I was not on the right road and had to find a way to get it turned around. Anna awoke and asked, "Where the hell are we?" I told her what I was trying to do and what our current situation was. She said, "You need to turn this thing around!"

"I know!"

The road was in a depression and I would have to fight to get it out to higher ground to get turned around. I saw a good spot to do this, punched the accelerator and whipped the RV ninety degrees as I climbed out of the depression. I didn't know an RV could do something like that, but it did. Once I had it on higher ground, there was no mud so I was able to get positioned to drop back into the depression going the opposite direction; which I did. When I dropped in, the whole RV tipped to the right and Zachary rolled out of his bed onto the floor. What was funny is that he didn't say anything, crawled back into his bed and went back to sleep. Anna sat with me until I made it back to the paved road and told me to stop right there so we could get some sleep. I had no argument.

The next morning I made some coffee while the others slept, then went outside to see just where we were. Just then, the only car I had seen since I got off the Interstate the night before came driving up, so I flagged him down to ask for directions to the marker. His response was, "Why the hell would anybody want to go there?" I laughed and told him what I had planned for the night before, and my plans for that morning to visit the highpoint of Nebraska. He chuckled and told me how to get to both places. We talked a little more before he took off. I jumped in the driver seat of the RV, started it up, and got us to the tri-state marker within two minutes. I was a lot closer than I thought and had just missed the correct road the night before by only one half of a mile. After I explained to my family where we were, we took some photos *and headed to Panorama Point which was only a few short miles away. Once we got there, I again told my family what it was, how I had been there twice before, some of my other highpointing adventures, and so-on. Anna cooked us up some great breakfast burritos; we took a couple photos, and headed off for South Dakota. This was Zachary's second highpoint (his first being Georgia), and Caitlyn's first and only. What a great trip that was.*

My children Caitlyn and Zachary standing on Panorama Point

Chapter 10
- The Santa Monica Freeway

I Picked Mike up at his house pretty late in the evening, and within minutes we found ourselves heading east on the Santa Monica Freeway (Interstate 10) for the long drive all the way across America. This freeway was basically going to be our home for the next couple days, and we were both a little less than enthused about it. We just wanted to get our butts to Florida as soon as we could in order to start seizing our next horde of peaks. I drove to Blythe, California, and then Mike drove from Blythe to Tucson, Arizona. I took over and drove to El Paso, Texas, and then he drove to Sonora, Texas. I got us to Houston, Texas, and he drove to Gulfport, Mississippi. After that, I got us to the massive, towering peak of Florida. What a long haul that was. We made it from Mike's driveway in Manhattan Beach, California to Britton Hill, Florida in just 32 hours. That has got to be some kind of record. I also never realized just how large the state of Texas really was. We were able to cross entire states on a single tank of gas, sometimes two! But it took almost four tanks to cross Texas. I thought we would never get across it! Also, all of those times we switched driving was when we were gassing up. We had finally got it worked out to where we did this to stay alert and get plenty of rest. This was a lesson learned from our previous mega-driving road trips.

While driving across the whole state of New Mexico, Mike and I drew up some blueprints for a fort that I was going to build for my kids in my back yard when I got back. Being the Engineers that we were, I think we did over design it just a little.

181

It was going to be built to last. There was also this one point in Texas when we were getting pretty hungry which meant it was time again to find a Subway Sandwich Shop. As we blew past Sonora, Texas at about eighty miles per hour, we realized the next major city capable of even having a remote chance of possessing a Subway was several hours away. Not to mention the next off-ramp past Sonora was in fact ten or twelve miles away from our present position. We made a command decision at that point and pulled our first U-turn on an Interstate. It didn't matter very much since there were no other cars for miles in either direction.

We went back to Sonora, gassed up (both the car and ourselves), then it was my shift to get us to the next fueling stop in Houston. As I pulled out of the parking lot and got us back onto the Santa Monica Freeway, I punched the accelerator going up the ramp and said out loud, "BwuaaaaaaaAAAAAA!" imitating what I wished my car really sounded like. Mike got a real kick out of that, so much so that he actually reminded me of it many years later when he took me out for a Subway sandwich on my 50th birthday.

I had fallen asleep while Mike was driving the leg from Houston to Gulfport. I remember waking up somewhere in Texas and asking him if we were in Louisiana yet. He said that we were still in Texas and had a ways to go before we crossed the border. I responded with, "Dang! Well, wake me when we cross the Mississippi River." as I quickly drifted back into my slumber. The next thing I remember was Mike waking me up. The car was parked and the motor was off. I looked outside and we were parked at a gas station shrouded in fog. "Where are we?" I asked in a sleepy voice while rubbing my eyes and looking around in puzzlement.

"Gulfport," Mike responded with his usual grin.

"Wait. Isn't Gulfport in Mississippi?"

"Yep!"

"Well, what happened to Louisiana?"

"It's back that way," as Mike pointed west, still giving me the grin.

"What the hell?" I said as I sat up straight in my seat still looking around trying to figure things out.

"How's it goin' eh!?! You slept through the entire state of Louisiana!"

"How is that possible? When did we cross the Mississippi River? Man! I must had been really knocked out."

"Yep! You were! You never even flinched after you fell back asleep in Texas."

"Damn!"

I got out of the car to stretch a little before I crawled back in behind the wheel. Mike went inside the station to pay and came back out with two large cups of coffee (not free this time). I took a couple big swigs, started the car, got us back onto the Santa Monica Freeway heading east, and the next stop would be the lofty summit of Florida.

Oh, and I did end up building a good strong fort for my kids that following year. Mike actually gave me a lot of the supplies for it. Unfortunately a California wildfire took it in 2006. C'est la vie.

Florida Britton Hill
345' December 29, 1996

It had just rained before we got to Britton Hill, and the air was crisp and clear and full of aromas that you can only experience in Florida on a day like this; kind of a mixture of both floral and fungus. I had tons of family in Florida, and spent just about every summer of my childhood there. If you had spent as much time in Florida as I had, you would know exactly what I am talking about.

The terrain around the peak was much like that of Alabama, and since the Alabama border was only about fifteen hundred feet from where we were standing, that made plenty of sense. We walked about fifty feet from our car to the summit and took our photos. Because Mike had been there before, he shared some of his previous experiences with me, including how after he left my dad's place when I flew home to be with Anna, he had to pull over in a truck stop to get some sleep before he killed somebody from fatigue. He had kept up the same pace after I left, and not having a second person to share in the driving really wore on him.

"Well enough of this!" I said, "We need to get to my dad's for dinner, and then bag Alabama by tonight!"

"Damn right! Let's go!"

Before we left I pulled out a couple oranges for Mike and I to munch on before we peeled-out ourselves. I threw my peels into a wastebasket and heard something move around inside. I peered into the can and to my surprise there was a huge possum sleeping in there. Or at least he *was* sleeping until I woke him. He wasn't a very happy camper and gave us a mean sounding hisssss. That's all it took for me to leave him alone. He was a big guy too. I just had to take a picture of him.

When we got back into the car, I threw my guidebook up onto the dash. As soon as I did this, Mike asked, "Why do you keep your book in a Ziploc bag? Is it to keep it dry? HA HA HA!!!"

"You are never going to let me live that one down are you?"

"How's it goin' eh?!"

We hit the road and found ourselves in Alabama within a minute. We stopped for gas right outside of Montgomery, Alabama where I took the opportunity to call Anna to tell her that we had safely made it to the other side of the country and that we had already bagged our first peak. Her response was, "You guys are nuts! You only left here just two nights ago! How is that possible?" I also gave my dad a call to give him heads-up that we would be arriving at his house in a couple of hours. As I was on the phone with my dad, Mike went inside to pay-up. When he came out of the store, he had a big friggin smile, held his coffee mug high above his head and shouted, "How's it goin' eh!?". How was he always able to do this? When we got to Atlanta, we ordered a couple pizzas, I changed the oil in my car (one of Anna's conditions for borrowing her car), we watched Mission Impossible (another lousy movie), and at about 6:30

PM on 29 Dec, we were headed back west to the high country of Alabama.

In total, I had summited Britton Hill twice:
Climb #1 was for score and was as just told here in Chapter 10.
Climb #2 is as told in Chapter 16.

48 Mountains

Alabama Cheaha Mountain
2,407' December 28, 1996

It took about two hours to get from my dad's house to the highpoint in Alabama. It was about 8:30PM, dark of course, and very foggy. The last part of the one-way road leading to the peak was blocked by a chain, so we had to walk the last couple hundred feet to the summit. There were a couple of old looking buildings and a radio tower up there. One of the buildings looked sort of like a church and was totally made of stone. We took our photos through the fog, and it was back to the car to head on out to Mississippi.

The route to this highpoint was a one-way, narrow road that looped around the mountain. From the main parking lot, it was about 1/4 mile to the peak. When we left the peak Mike suggested that we go back the way we came because the other way would take us way out of the way. It was late and there was nobody else around, so why not? We started going the wrong way on this one-way road, and then all of a sudden out of nowhere, a pickup truck came up the road and stopped about fifty feet in front of us. We backed off the road to let him pass, but he just sat there. About a minute had passed when this person turned on his high beams and continued to sit there blinding us. This was starting to get a little frustrating and unnerving. "What's this guy doing?" I asked. Mike flashed him with the high beams a couple times, but he continued to just sit there and block the road. We had eventually had enough and turned the car around to drive back the other way. This person then proceeded to follow us all the way around the mountain until we got back onto the main highway leading away from the mountain. It's just kind of spooky being in unfamiliar places in the middle of the night when something like that happens.

Once we left Cheaha Mountain, it was now off to Mississippi. Again, just like most if not all the states in the south, road maps almost serve no purpose, except maybe to remind you that you are in fact still in that particular state. We couldn't find the road that would take us to Interstate 20, and ended up in Talladega, Alabama. We were on a tight schedule as usual, and this cost us some precious time. We eventually found the Interstate, got to Birmingham where we gassed-up in a 'really nice' part of town, and then headed north on Interstate 65 towards the Mississippi highpoint.

It was about 10:00PM when I came over a rise in the road and saw the occasional set of brake lights come on a couple miles out in the distance ahead of me; all seemingly to coming on at the same exact same location. This was the usual indicator that a cop was near. As I drove a little further, a car approaching in the opposite direction flashed his high beams at me twice which *is* the signal in the south warning you of police presence up ahead. I took it down from 80 to 65 and pulled into the slow lane to mix in with the other cars there. I pissed off the idiot behind me who proceeded to get into the fast lane and blast down the highway at full speed. I was laughing as I watched him pass the cop sitting in the center divider. This guy then slowed back down and dove into the slow lane between some cars just like what I did. The cop then pulled onto the freeway just as I passed him with all of his lights flashing. There were eight of us all going the same speed in the slow lane, and the cop now had to guess which one of us it was that blew past him just a few seconds earlier. He proceeded to pull over the wrong guy. At 8-1 odds, I was sure glad it wasn't me. Now that that was behind us, I sped back up to eighty miles per hour to make up some time.

"Damn you AAA! When are you going to have some decent road maps of the south!?" I knew I had to get off the Interstate around Decatur, but we missed our off-ramp either because the ramp wasn't clearly marked, or the map was wrong; or probably a combination of the two. A sign stated, "Next exit ten miles." We pulled our second U-turn on an Interstate right there on the spot and got back on track. Mike had been sleeping since we filled the car with gas back in Birmingham, and slept though everything. After our next highpoint in Mississippi, it would be another long, dull drive all the way back across the country for the second time in two days.

In total, I had stood atop Cheaha Mountain two times:

Climb #1 was for score and was as just told here in Chapter 10.

Climb #2 was with my dad and little brother Chris back on February 16, 2000. I call him my little brother because he is five years my junior, but much bigger and a few inches taller than me which make people look at me funny when I introduce him this way. My dad had been transferred to Atlanta, Georgia back in 1989 after the company he had worked for since the 1960s had been gobbled up by another larger company based in Atlanta and moved him there. He always disliked the south and decided to move back home to California once he had the opportunity. My brother and I flew out there, helped him pack his rented moving van, and readied for our cross-country trip that would start early the next morning. Not only had we loaded all of his worldly possessions that were neatly packed in boxes into the van, but we also had a huge 100 year old upright piano packed in there as well as two full-sized Yamahas which were the same size and weight as the piano. Those three items alone were a lot of fun loading up the narrow, flimsy, aluminum ramp in the middle of the night.

Now when you are travelling across the country, not for pleasure, but moving a whole house, the only thing you really want is to get it over with as soon as possible. We planned to do a couple of highpoints along the way back across the country since they were located along the route we were taking. Cheaha Mountain would be the first one, and since it was only a couple of hours from Atlanta, we were up there in no time at all. It was nothing like last time I was there when the mystery vehicle was menacing both Mike and I until we got off the mountain. It was daylight this time, and there were tourists around. I could actually see what it looked like this time since it had been so foggy and dark the last time I was there. I reminded my dad that he was still a highpointer due to

191

climbing Georgia and Tennessee's highpoints with me (Chapter 4), and now he had a third highpoint under his belt. I also told Chris that he too was now a highpointer. My dad responded with, "All right!", while Chris' response was basically, "No thanks".

When I was there previously with Mike, we used the sign as proof we were at the highpoint because it was so dark and foggy. The true highpoint was a large rock behind the building that you can faintly see in the previous photo. We thought that taking photos on the rock that night would have came out terrible, so we opted to take our photos at the sign instead.

My Dad & Chris standing on the Alabama Highpoint

Mississippi Woodall Mountain
806' December 30, 1996

Mike must have been really out of it. With the commotion of the cop car, me pulling another Interstate U-turn, and stopping for the occasional draining of the lizard, he never even stirred. When we were within a couple miles of the peak, I kept stopping, turning on the dome light, and consulting my trusty highpoints book and a map for directions. I had to keep turning on the light because it was the middle of the night again. The last mile to the peak was a very bumpy and steep dirt road. When I got to the top of the mountain, I stopped right in front of the sign stating that we had made it to Mississippi's highpoint. I wanted so bad to startle Mike somehow, but I know how payback is a bitch, so I quietly woke him. He jumped up, looked around and said, "OK! We're here!"

It had just rained prior to our arrival, so the ground was very wet and muddy, and the outside temperature was very cold. It was also very dark, so there was really nothing to see. The maps showed this area to be heavily wooded, but we really couldn't see a thing. There was a radio tower at the top, and we could actually hear people talking through the wires; that was very strange. We took our photos, gave our highpoint hugs, and

it was now time to go all of the way back across the country yet
again.

As soon as we hit the pavement, Mike was out again just
like that. He slept all the way into Arkansas. Not your Kansas,
or my Kansas... Ar-kansas. I woke him as we drove past Elvis
Presley's home Graceland, and he was out like a light bulb after
that. It was very foggy from Mississippi, Through Memphis,
Tennessee, across the Mississippi River, and well into Arkansas.
Visibility was about 1/4 mile, which wasn't that bad. It was
time to gas-up the car, so as we were approaching an off-ramp I
started looking off to the right through the fog to see if I could
spot a gas station. It was just at that moment when we hit a wall
of fog so thick that I couldn't see the lines on the road. And I
was going about 75 miles per hour! I slowed down quickly, but
not too quickly because I knew there was a car right behind me
somewhere. If there were cars stopped in that fog when I went
in, we would have been toast. I was also glad the car behind me
was paying attention to the situation as well.

I safely got off the Interstate and pulled into the only station
there. "Mike, wake up. It's your turn to drive." After we gassed

up and took off, I tried to get some sleep, but it was difficult to relax knowing that we were driving through that stuff. I was finally in a good sleep when the car swerved all of a sudden, and it felt like we were going off-road. I sat up and shouted, "What's going on?!" All I could see was fog and an 18-wheeler right outside my window. I thought Mike had fallen asleep and we were going off the freeway or something. It turned out that some idiot Arkansas driver wouldn't let Mike over to make our interchange, so he had to cross the gore point going 55 miles per hour. The truck that was next to us was blocking the view of an Arkansas state trooper who never saw what happened. It was hard, but I did eventually get back to sleep after all of that commotion. Because of this, Mike is now known as, "Gore Point Gauthier." By the way, his last name is pronounced, "Go-shay." Why am I telling you this two thirds into the book? Why not?

The next time we stopped was in Okemah, Oklahoma, where Mike told me that it had been foggy across the entire state of Arkansas. He also told me that he had spent most of his time that night spreading maps all over the inside of the car and at one point had me completely blanketed in them. I asked why, and he said he was trying to better calculate when we would get to Laughlin. Boredom does make us do strange things, especially studying maps while driving down a foggy interstate at 75 miles per hour.

When we were driving through Oklahoma City, I saw a Waffle House and realized that the 'eggs and grits' content in my blood was really low, so I pulled off the freeway for some southern sustenance. You never go into the south without getting some real grits. After our hearty breakfast it was back onto the Interstate. Somewhere between Oklahoma City and Amarillo, TX, I ended up following an 18 wheeler going over ninety miles per hour. I was drafting him, and as a result we got some of the best gas mileage of our entire trip. There was another car with a lady driver right behind us the whole way doing the same thing. We all did this for over 100 miles. We were like a bullet train blasting down the Interstate. Every time the truck switched lanes, we were right behind him. I finally pulled off in Amarillo for gas, and our truck and caboose were gone. The lady waved at us as she went by. She was from Colorado. Hopefully she finds this book someday and realizes it is her that I am talking about.

We drove through the panhandle of Texas and through New Mexico into Albuquerque. We had to stop again for gas, and it was yet another opportunity to fill our stomachs with Subway Sandwiches. Sounds like I am always plugging this company, but we honestly cannot get enough of these things. After looking for some time, we couldn't locate a Subway, so we settled for 'Burger Sling'. It was my turn to drive, and I took us from Albuquerque to Flagstaff, AZ. Mike filled up the car while I took the opportunity to make another phone call to Anna. I was just in a pair of jeans and a T-shirt with my blue jacket. I hadn't been in cold like that for a long time and had to 'cut' Anna short so I could get back into the warm car. She couldn't believe that we had already come all the way back across the country and got two more highpoints in the process.

We got to Laughlin about 1:00AM and gambled for a couple hours. After losing a few bucks on the slot machines, I ended up walking aimlessly through the casino always within earshot of Mike's, "Yo 'leven!" I went over to watch him play craps for a while, and then we departed for home. Boy was I tired, and it was my turn to drive. I got us to Barstow, and Mike got us home.

During our cross-country excursion, we started planning for our New England trip that was to occur sometime in the middle of the following year. I always loved planning out our trips. Like I said earlier, planning these things is one-third the fun. Getting to them and actually doing them are the other two thirds. This trip was a total logistical nightmare to plan, but ended up being a really great trip due to all of our pre-planning. In the initial preparation stages, I just figured we could make a huge loop out of it; land in Boston, just circle around the states to get the peaks, and fly home.

The way I saw it, we would do:

Rhode Island
Connecticut
Delaware
New Jersey
Massachusetts
New York
Vermont
New Hampshire
Maine

This was going to be no problem at all. I couldn't wait to get home to start looking at maps and get things started.

In total, I had visited Woodall Mountain twice:

Climb #1 was for score and was as just told here in Chapter 10. After I informed the Highpointers Club regarding our trip along the Santa Monica Freeway, this appeared in their following quarterly newsletter: "In pursuit of 3HPs (2 at night!!), John White and Mike Gauthier traveled 4,781 miles,,, in 80 hours!"

Climb #2 was again with my dad and Chris, and it was accomplished just hours after Cheaha Mountain in Alabama on February 16, 2000. Because I had not been there for several years, I forgot what the road leading to the summit was like. It was basically too late to make any changes as I was driving the rented moving van up the rutty, muddy, steep dirt road in the middle of the night. My dad and Chris were holding onto anything they could to keep from being bounced around the cab, and my dad kept reminding me about the heavy cargo we were carrying and wasn't sure if the flimsy rollup door in the back could hold it all in. We had no choice as I had no plans of backing this thing back down the mountain in the middle of the night. I just kept it full-throttle and plowed ahead until we reached the summit. The first thing we did when we got out of the truck was to make sure everything inside didn't come crashing through the back door on the way up. We carefully opened the door and everything looked good, but we could tell that the entire contents of the truck had shifted back towards the rear. "No worries!" I said. "It will all shift back to the front on the way back down!" with a huge smile on my face. My dad still tells this story from time to time.

The summit was a lot rougher looking this time around. It looked as if it had become the local teenage hangout. The sign I had my photo taken in front of just a few years prior was totally demolished, and all that was left was what you see in the photo below. Congrats to my dad for accomplishing his fourth highpoint, and for Chris for completing his second. One more and you receive the coveted Highpointers Club Five Peaks Patch pop!!!

Chapter 11
- The Logistical Nightmare

It was a darn good thing I decided to take a closer look at certain details when planning for the north east trip. Items like: Rhode Island's highpoint being on private property, and the owner being a grumpy old man who didn't like trespassers on his land. New Jersey's highpoint being open only from 8:00AM to 8:00PM. Connecticut's and New York's being somewhat difficult hikes through unfamiliar wooded areas (very easy to get lost in). The road leading to the Massachusetts highpoint only being open from late May through November 1. Vermont's being open only from 10:00AM to 5:00PM. There being only one way to cross from New York into Vermont in a car in that part of the country. New Hampshire's being closed all weekend due to an annual auto race taking place. It was only open for a few hours on Sunday. Maine's being open only from 6:00AM to 8:00PM. Not to mention all the numerous tolls and fees we had to pay everywhere. Many of the freeways were toll roads. You couldn't take a freeway, or cross a bridge without paying a toll. Most of the highpoint parking areas also required a fee of some sort; some of them costing as much as $21.00.

After I figured everything out, Mike and I got together for over two hours one evening to try and determine the best route to take on this expedition. We had to establish how we were going to get onto all of these mountains while they were open during the short amount of time we had scheduled to be in New England. We tried every scenario, and finally came up with one that was totally ridiculous to look at on a map, but it worked. Land in Boston, do MA, NY, VT, drive ALL THE WAY down to DE, do, NJ, CT, RI, drive ALL THE WAY up to ME, do NH, and return back to Boston. This probably increased our mileage by 75%, but it was the best way, the only way. It would have taken us five days to complete all of the highpoints of New England, but because of our planning and ingenuity, it only took us three. Take a good look at the map (next page) and see what we had to deal with to get all of the peaks. We had to go way north, then way south, then way north again, then back south to complete the trip. All in all, it was a lot of fun to plan.

48 Mountains

Just follow the arrows from Boston.

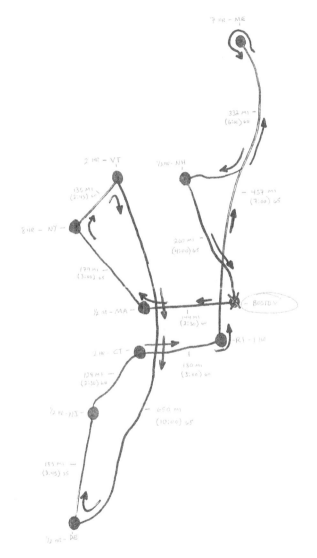

Delaware Ebright Azimuth
442' June 24, 1997

Five days before the trip, I was sent as a representative of my company to visit a supplier of ours in Delaware. I traveled with four other coworkers: (Teresa, Sylvia, LeAnna and Sean), and we all arrived in Washington D.C. early Sunday morning. We rented a minivan and did as much site seeing as we could before we drove up to Delaware to check into our hotel. I learned a very valuable lesson that day; never try to see all of Washington DC in one day. It's totally ridiculous to even try.

I did have one very cool experience while I was visiting the Vietnam Veteran's Memorial. I had a cousin by the name of Robert Lee White who was a Sergeant in the United States Army who died in Vietnam in 1965. Because I knew I was going to visit the wall, I brought a photo of him with me. When I found his name engraved in the wall, I had Teresa hold the photo by his name so I could take a photo. There were many people there all milling about, talking, touching the wall, etc. But when I took that photo, I remember the whole area becoming absolutely and eerily quiet. Everybody had stopped what they were doing to watch as I did this. I later asked the others why they thought this happened, and they told me that it was because the wall became incredibly real to everybody at that very moment. Like I said, very cool.

That night after we checked in to our hotel in Newark, Delaware, we all decided to see what was fun and exciting to do around town. Before we left the hotel, I told the others not to expect too much. I reminded them of that scene in *Wayne's World* when Wayne and Garth were pretending to visit fun places all over America like Hawaii, New York and Texas. When they pretended to be in Delaware, they both stopped what they were doing, gave a blank stare, and said in a monotone voice, "Hi... We're in Delaware." We asked around and it turned out that Wayne and Garth were absolutely correct. The only thing we found to do was to drive over the Delaware Memorial Bridge which goes from Delaware to New Jersey. As we were crossing the bridge, I said, "Hi... We're in Delaware." Everybody broke down laughing and then somebody suggested we go and find a place to get a drink.

We went on the hunt for a bar and could not locate one anywhere. After about thirty minutes of fruitless searching, I stopped and asked a man getting into his car if he knew where the closest one was.

"Sure," he replied. There is one right down this street next to the Wawa."

"What?" I replied.

The man pointed down the street and said, "There is one right down that way. You will find it next to the Wawa."

Sean replied, "Next to the what?"

"The Wawa."

"The Wawa?" I asked

The man paused, looked us over, and then said, "Y'all ain't from around here, are you?"

With that we all busted out laughing, including the man. We told him we were from California, and he explained to us that a Wawa was much like our 7-Eleven stores. We found the Wawa and then found the bar right where he told us it would be. Before we went into the bar, I took a photo of the Wawa for a memento. We laughed about that one for years.

The last full day of our trip, I talked everybody into going to Delaware's highpoint which was only about twenty minutes away from our hotel. I thought it would be cool to get this highpoint before I got it with Mike on the following Saturday. We all piled into our minivan, got to the highpoint within minutes, and I made highpointers out of the lot of them right there on the spot. We didn't spend much time there. We just took some photos under the highpoint sign, and then went off to find something to eat. None of them were even remotely interested in doing this when I initially asked, but they all thought it was pretty cool and a lot of fun afterwards. This all happened on a Tuesday.

The following Thursday back in California, I met Mike down at his girlfriend's house and she then took us to the airport. The flight from Los Angeles to Boston was pretty much uneventful... until our final approach. The aircraft hit some severe turbulence that made me very uneasy as well as the lady sitting next to me who started to panic and kept repeating, "Oh my God… Oh my God… Oh my God…" She wasn't helping my situation at all. I looked over at her and could see that she was visibly terrified. I put out my hand and she immediately grabbed it and held so tight that I heard my knuckles crack. She calmed down a bit and continued to tightly hold my hand until the plane touched down and left the runway. When she finally let go and the blood started flowing back through my hand, she turned to me and said, "Thank you so much, I'm so embarrassed."

"Don't worry about it," I responded. "I was just as nervous as you. We did each other a favor."

Mike and I went straight to Alamo to get our rental car after we retrieved our luggage. They had Mike's name on file this time. Mike carefully glanced over at me with a worried look and said, "Oh oh." under his breath. We thought we had been made due to how many miles we had been putting on their cars over the last several years. We were very surprised and relieved to learn that he wasn't on file for putting 4019 miles on a car on our south east trip, or for putting 5502 miles on a brand new car on our mid west trip, and not for putting 2985 miles on a car on our Texas / Nebraska trip. Nope. He was in their files because he was a frequent renter! Can you believe that? And not only that, he was now eligible to receive certain benefits and privileges with his frequent renter status. On top of that, they gave us another brand new car with only six miles on it again! I felt like going up to the clerk and asking, "Don't you know who this guy is? Isn't he on your 'most wanted' list or something? Isn't there a photo of him somewhere behind the counter?"

As soon as we picked up the car and left the airport, we immediately got stuck in traffic on the Massachusetts Turnpike, which also turned out to be the first of several toll roads we would encounter over the next few days. It took us over an hour just to get through the Ted Williams Tunnel. What a way to get our next grand adventure started.

Massachusetts Mount Greylock
3941' June 26, 1997

It was supposed to be a three hour drive from Logan International Airport to the highpoint of Massachusetts, but because of the airport traffic and getting lost in Boston, as well as the numerous toll booths and the slow winding roads, it took more like five hours before we arrived at the summit. I recall it being a very dark night, maybe due to cloud cover or for some other reason. The peak was also located in a very rural part of the state, so not too many city lights to make the night time sky glow. I got very excited when I first spotted the lighted beacon located on top of the highpoint way out in the distance through the trees. I tried pointing it out to Mike a few times until he finally saw it as well. The light was actually a huge lit globe perched on top of a memorial dedicated to our American Veterans of World War I. We were still about thirty miles away and could see the beacon as clear as day.

It was about 1:00AM when we finally reached the peak. It was very cold and windy up there. We parked the car and rushed up the stairs leading to the summit. Mike told me not to waste much time because we were exceedingly behind schedule at this point and needed to make it up anywhere we could before we got to New York's highpoint. We quickly took our pictures, ran back down the stairs, literally jumped back into the car for warmth, and then headed off to New York. As we were driving away from Mount Greylock, I realized that I didn't spend any time reflecting on my highpointing success up there. I felt like I was starting to take it all for granted. I was forgetting what I was doing, why I was doing it, how lucky I was to be doing it, and that I was doing it with such a great friend as Mike. I thought about all of this and just figured it was because the peaks we had done lately were so simple and unimpressive. I promised myself from that point on to be more attentive to what I was doing and to appreciate the whole adventure more. My first test of this would be on top of New York the following morning.

The roads through the backcountry of Massachusetts and New York were unbelievably slow, and navigating through them took a lot more time than I had figured. I always assumed that fifty-five miles per hour on two lane roads was good enough when I planned out the trip, but for New England I now suggest forty-five miles per hour. This poor calculation had put us a couple hours behind on our very tight schedule. The reason for the time concern was the fact that we had to get to Vermont's peak the next day before it closed. And we still had to climb New York's highpoint before that which was going to take us at least eight hours. And we still needed to get some sleep somewhere in the mix. We drove all night to Mount Marcy and got a couple hours of shuteye at the trailhead before we started our hike the next morning.

New York Mount Marcy
5344' June 27, 1997

We woke up early to a very cold morning and started our hike about 6:00AM. We didn't get much sleep that night because we had a time concern regarding Vermont's highpoint and needed to get Mount Marcy as quickly as we possibly could. The first three miles of the trail were fairly decent and we made some really good time. It was the remaining four miles that really slowed us down tremendously. The trail became extremely muddy, steep and very rocky. There was so much mud on this trail that wood planks and logs had been placed everywhere over the years to prevent people from having to walk in the muck. Some of the wood planks were so rotted that I would sink right through it as I stepped on them. The last mile was especially difficult due to the trail just being seemingly paved in huge protruding boulders. We walked the entire way to the top without jackets, but the last few hundred yards got very cold very suddenly. It was kind of strange actually: the whole way to the top was nice, and breezy, but when we rounded this one bend near the top, the wind and freezing cold almost knocked us over. Mike was about one hundred feet in front of me during the last mile or so, and I caught up to him waiting for me just before that bend. "What's up?" I asked.

"Walk up that way about twenty feet," as he pointed up the trail.

"Why? And why are you putting on your jacket? It's nice up here."

"Just do it. You'll see," he said with a smile.

"Why? Is the Swedish Bikini Team up there waiting for us or something?"

"HA HA! I wish! Just go around that bend and check it out."

I did as he instructed, and when I took that last step and almost fell over backwards from the fierce, freezing wind… "Holy crap!" I yelled as I quickly leaped back a few steps for protection. Mike started laughing so hard and said, "I know! I experienced the same thing and just wanted you to share in the experience! How's it goin' eh!? HA HA HA!"

"You slime bag! You could have warned me or something!"

"Then it wouldn't have been as funny! HA HA HA!"

"Damn that was cold!"

I put on my jacket while still grumbling to Mike under my breath, and then we continued up the trail trying to shield ourselves as best we could from the bitter wind. The wind only lasted about one hundred yards and then died away as we approached the summit. When the summit came into view, I could see the clouds blowing over and around the mountain. There was a sea of thin, fast moving clouds and the very peak of Mount Marcy protruding up through them looked like an island in the mist. It was an incredible thing to observe. When I reached the summit and stood on top, the clouds were actually blowing around my feet like as if I were standing in a stream of vapor (yes, I know clouds are made of vapor). They also blew around the sides of the peak, and then just dissipated into nothingness. The Native Americans used to call Mount Marcy "Tahawus", which means "Cloud Splitter", and this is exactly what it was doing. It was so amazing and beautiful to witness.

On the top we met a young man who called himself, "The Keeper of the Mountain." He was a young college student who belonged to a small organization that made sure people were informed on certain matters pertaining to the local mountains. He also enlightened us on how to not damage the environment, and how to stay safe during our visit. He said that he was a volunteer and stayed up there for weeks at a time. I felt that he should go out and get a job.

While we were up there, I awarded Mike with a pin from the Highpointers Club. The award was for hiking thirty peaks with at least five of the peaks in each of the four designated geographical zones: The West, The Southeast, The Mid-West and the Northeast. At this point Mike actually had thirty-eight peaks under his belt, but he needed this last one in the Northeast to qualify him for the pin. I wouldn't get this same pin until I completed New Mexico someday in the future. We spent enough time up there to have a few munchies which we shared with Mr. Keeper, and then we were off to Vermont before it closed.

Vermont Mount Mansfield
4,393' June 27, 1997

Driving away from Mount Marcy, I noticed just how very beautiful that area of the country really was. We couldn't see any of the countryside the night before, but now there it was in its total splendor. The mountain is located near Lake Placid, which was the location for the 1976 Winter Olympics. I could see why they chose this setting to show off what America had to offer. It was all just simply picturesque. The ski jumps from those Olympics were visible out in the distance and a pretty awesome sight to see.

Part of the planning for this trip was trying to figure out the quickest, most direct route from Mount Marcy in New York to Mount Mansfield in Vermont. Between those two states lies the seemingly impassable Lake Champlain. Why nobody had ever built more bridges across that 125 mile long lake in America's over 230 year history is beyond me. All of our trips were planned before Al Gore invented the Internet, so I always had to plan them using very unreliable AAA maps, just as what happened to me on my southeastern trips. It seemed at first that we would either have to go all the way to the Canadian border to make a crossing, or go a good portion back towards Mount

216

Greylock in Massachusetts. I finally found us a bridge, the only bridge crossing the lake some fifty miles out of our way.

We arrived at the entrance gate to Mount Mansfield with just one hour to spare. After the lady in the toll booth collected our fee, she told us that she would have to lock the gate with us on the inside after she left at 5:00PM. At last, the "Logistical Nightmare" was starting to become a reality. This meant that we would need to get to the top and back down to the gate in one hell of a hurry. The road took us up to the ridge of the mountain, and then we had to walk about three miles along the ridge to the peak and back. The trail was very rocky and muddy in places, but it was a very direct route and we reached the summit in record time. Guess who we found sitting on the top? Another "Keeper of the Mountain".

It was a grand vista from the top. You could see Mount Marcy (the mountain we just came from) to the southwest, and Mount Washington (the mountain we were going to 'summit' in a few days) out in the distance to the east of us. We had zero time to waste since we needed to get back through the gate before the lady locked it, so we quickly took our photos and high-tailed it back to the car. I remember there was a gentleman sitting on the summit playing a guitar, and I could hear him for quite a distance as we hurriedly scrambled back to the parking lot. We drove back down the mountain as fast as we could to a locked gate just like the lady had told us. We 'Missed it by that much'. Mike and I looked at each other, and I think I let out an expletive or two before Mike pointed out a hand written sign posted on the gate stating where we could find the key that would let us out. We located the key, and then headed out on our long detour to Delaware some 650 miles to the south of us. It was ironic that we were so near to Mount Washington in New Hampshire, and we had to skip it for now in order for our plan to succeed. We were about two hours behind schedule at this point, but I knew we would be able to make up some time during the journey to our nation's first state. We really had to keep to the schedule on this trip. We had absolutely no room for error and couldn't risk getting locked in or out of any more highpoints on this trip.

We were getting pretty hungry after all of our recent hiking and driving, so of course we couldn't go all that way to Delaware without some Subway sustenance. I remember wanting one of their sandwiches badly, but I don't remember if we ever found one of their shops. I think we ended up getting some very unhealthy munchies during one of our refueling stops. We had been constantly going since our flight arrived in Boston, and I still had no real sleep since the night before I left California. I was so tired that I slept half the way to Delaware. Mike had driven from Vermont down into Connecticut and fatigue finally caught up with him as well, so we went ahead and switched places between refueling stops. Even though we had it all worked out to switch places only during fueling stops, there were times like this when it became necessary to change places.

It was about midnight and was now my shift to get us the rest of the way to Delaware. I drove over the George Washington Bridge in New York, and then through the entire state of New Jersey from top to bottom. I then crossed from New Jersey into Delaware via "The Delaware Memorial Bridge" for the second time in just a few days on two different trips. About the midpoint of the bridge, I said quietly to myself, "Hi... I'm in Delaware." It was all a little surreal and I did laugh to myself about it.

I was really tired myself at this point and not feeling too great. I think it was all the coffee and sunflower seeds I had consumed during the night. On the plus-side, we were about two hours ahead of schedule now. We had somehow made up four hours on this leg of the trip. Mike was sound asleep and I needed to find a place to get a couple hours of shut-eye myself. The hotel I had stayed at just a week prior was only a few miles from our location, so I took us there and we slept in the car in the parking lot in full view of the room I had just occupied. Again, kind of weird. Mike opened his eyes for a few seconds after I parked and asked where we were. I told him, "Delaware," and he said "Good" as he quickly drifted back to sleep.

The next day, the whole day, I felt simply awful; my stomach was queasy. I had a strenuous hike in Connecticut to do at the end of the day, and the 'grand daddy' of this trip Katahdin to do the following day. I wasn't really looking forward to doing them feeling the way I was. I felt like I was ready to toss my cookies at any moment. We drove to the Delaware highpoint (again, weird), 'bagged' it on June 28, 1997 for a second time, and it was off to New Jersey.

Mike at Delaware's Highpoint. "Hi… we're in Delaware…"

In total, I had now stood atop Ebright Azimuth twice as just told in this chapter. I did not have a photo taken of me on my second visit with Mike.

New Jersey High Point
1,803' June 28, 1997

I asked Mike to drive to New Jersey's highpoint so I could get some more rest, and to somehow get myself to feeling a little better. I was feeling much worse than the night before and kept a plastic bag at the ready just in case. I told Mike not to worry, and that I was still 100% committed to completing all of the highpoints on this trip. He told me to just take it easy and get plenty of rest. Connecticut's demanding highpoint was several hours away and we still had New Jersey's very easy one to complete first. I had plenty of time. Before we got going, I had Mike pull into a small convenience store so I could get a pint of ice-cold milk. I am not much of a milk drinker these days, but there was a time when I swore by the stuff and I knew I needed to get some into me as quickly as possible to start the healing process. It did make my stomach feel a lot better within minutes, but my body was still fighting something. Looking back, I think it was just fatigue mixed with a lot of bad coffee and crappy food that put the zap on me.

We drove through Pennsylvania, and then to the very top northeast corner of New Joyzee (that's how the people there pronounced it anyway). I always pictured in my mind that New Jersey, New York, Connecticut and Rhode Island was one big

221

massive city that was spread out across the countryside like Los Angeles is. I quickly learned that this was not the case at all. I couldn't believe how much untouched country there still is out there. You can be thirty minutes out of a major city, and still be in the countryside. If you're thirty minutes out of Los Angeles, you're still in Los Angeles.

New Jersey (what I saw of it) was a very beautiful place; lots of forest, and very green. The 220 foot monument on the highpoint looked a lot like a miniature Washington Monument back in Washington D.C., and the view from the top was gorgeous. There were trees and lakes as far as I could see. I could also see New York and Pennsylvania from up there.

After we left the peak, I had Mike stop the car next to a lake in full view of the monument we had just stood on top of. I took some photos, and then awarded Mike with another pin from the Highpointers Club. This pin was for completing *any* 40 highpoints. This peak was his 41st. I had forgotten to award it to him in Delaware because of how I was feeling at the time. I wouldn't get my 40 Peak Pin until I completed New Hampshire at the end of the trip.

I still wasn't feeling well there in New Jersey, and started really working on my psyche to prepare myself for Connecticut. I told Mike that there was a small chance that I would be skipping Connecticut because of how I was feeling. But I also added that I was still 100% committed to the goal and would give it a shot even if I thought there was only a 1% chance of my making it to the top. I wanted this… I needed this. I was also feeling some pressure because this was the first time in my 33 years that I would be in Connecticut, and who knew if I would ever get there again. I knew this was my only chance and I really needed to get this into my brain that I was going to do this mountain 'do or die'.

After we left New Jersey's highpoint, we immediately headed into Connecticut for our next conquest. We had to stop for gas on the way, and learned that they still do it the old way in some places. They fill out the little slip, go to the back of the car to take the license number, have you sign it, give you your carbon copies, etc. Mike asked, "You guys still do it that old way? The man replied, "Yeah. Were a little behind the times here in New Jersey, but that's the way we like it." I admired that.

Connecticut Mount Frissell
2,380' June 28, 1997

We knew we had found the trailhead when we came to the primitive fence that divided Connecticut from Massachusetts. We were deep in the woods on a lonely dirt road, and there was another car parked there that meant there were other people on the mountain. Mike parked the car, looked at me and asked, "Well? You gonna do it?"

Still feeling totally crappy and unsure, I looked at him and said apprehensively, "OK, let's do it."

We both got out of the car and I was unpleasantly surprised to find that the air was hot, still, and very muggy. This did not sit well with me due to how I was feeling. I opened the trunk and got what I needed for the hike which consisted of a map, a scarf, and a water bottle. Mike wanted to change his clothes, so I slowly walked fifty feet across the Massachusetts state line, and then back to the car in Connecticut continually telling myself that I was going to do this.

The trail turned out to be totally awful. It was as if somebody said, "We need a trail to go straight from the bottom of this mountain to the top," and somebody took it way too literal. This trail went straight from where the car was parked to the top of Mount Frissell. Straight! No curves... straight!

224

Straight up and straight down cliffs and rocks. No switch backs, no going around tough spots, nothing. It was a good thing there were no large trees in the way or we would have had to climb over them as well. The elevation gain of this mountain is 833 feet per mile, which is pretty darn steep. The trail even went over a smaller mountain, down five hundred feet in elevation into a valley, and then back up to Mount Frissell. The elevation gain was probably more like 1071 feet per mile per my calculations. This was a really tough climb, one of the toughest I had done in a very long time.

This highpoint is very unique as it is the only highpoint in the country that you have to actually walk down to. We parked our car in Connecticut, walked north along the dirt road a couple hundred feet into Massachusetts, and then hiked west utilizing the trail from hell along the state line for a little over a mile up to the summit of Mount Frissell which is actually in Massachusetts. Then from that point, we hiked south down from the summit for a few hundred yards back into Connecticut, and then west along another trail for a couple hundred feet until we found the highpoint. Connecticut's highpoint is actually on the side of Mount Frissell. Connecticut does have a highest mountain called Bear Mountain which is only a mile from Mount Frissell. It stands at 2,316 feet, but is not the state's actual "highpoint". In the photo of me touching Connecticut's highpoint, I am actually sitting in Massachusetts, and technically not only am I touching Connecticut's highpoint, but I am also touching the state line. All kind of bizarre, but that's just the way it is.

I felt awful the whole way up to Connecticut's highpoint. I look at the photo of me taken at the summit and can see it plain as day. I just took the whole climb slow and steady and eventually made it to the highpoint. After we started heading back up to the top of Mount Frissell, I all of a sudden started feeling good again. I felt my energy coming back as well as my motivation. I had just completed my 37th highpoint and I think subconsciously this is where my boost came in to play. I was back! I told Mike the news and he responded with, "That's weird."

"I know, right?"

On the way up the mountain earlier during the climb, we had run into another hiker on his way down. He was up there just hanging out, and didn't even go to the Connecticut highpoint. We couldn't figure that one out. On our way back down, Mike found the man's water bottle hanging from a branch that hung over the trail. This branch had stealthily snagged this guys bottle without him even noticing. We tried to catch up to him, but he had a good thirty minute head start on us and we never found him. Mike got himself a nice, new water bottle that afternoon and still uses it to this day. When we got back to the car, we were absolutely soaked from all of the humidity. We changed out of our damp clothes, and were off to the dramatic and suspense-filled 812 foot highpoint of Rhode Island.

As we crossed the Connecticut / Rhode Island state line, Mike asked, "Do you know how Connecticut originally got its name?"

"Nope."

"Well, when the first settlers arrived in this area, a woman looked out across the land and asked, 'I wonder what they call this new land?' A local doctor thought he heard the woman ask, 'Where can I get this cut stitched-up in my hand?' The doctor yelled out, 'Miss! I can connect-a-cut!" and that is how Connecticut got its name."

I looked over at Mike and said, "Did I just fall for that again?"

Mike looked over at me with his wide-eyed grin and started laughing.

Now, I have never been the kind of person that would *knowingly* put myself into any kind of danger. I also remember after climbing Backbone Mountain in Maryland saying that, "I never wanted to go through something like that again. No more hiking on private property for me. Never again." Well, here I was getting ready to do it again.

Rhode Island Jerimoth Hill
812' June 28, 1997

This peak was, and will always be the most planned-out, covert, and suspenseful hike of all my highpoints. This highpoint was only accessible by crossing through private property, and the landowner was affectionately known by the Highpointers Club as, "The Jerimoth Madman." This person had physically attacked people who crossed his property to get to the highpoint. He had even been known to draw a gun on an entire group of boy scouts and made them lie face down on his property until the police arrived. As crappy as it all seemed, he actually had this right.

Mike and I came to the conclusion that we had to do this highpoint. In order to achieve our goal of standing on top of every peak in the nation, we had to actually stand on top of every peak in the nation. There was no other way of looking at it. What would I tell my kids? That I did 47 of the 48 highpoints, and I missed Rhode Island's by only a couple hundred feet because there was a crazy man in the way? I made up my mind that I wasn't going to let that happen. The Highpointers Club did state that where his driveway met the road could be considered as the highpoint due to the dire circumstances. Mike and I had discussed this situation on several occasions and concluded that when we got there, we were going in no matter the circumstances.

We arrived in front of his property right at dusk. We had to do this one without his knowledge, so like idiots we parked right in front of his house next to his driveway. I looked over at his house and saw his garage open and a TV on through an open window. Unfortunately this meant that he was home. This was a very thickly wooded area, so I hoped he wouldn't see our car and us sneaking our way to the highpoint. I took a photo of our car next to the sign showing that we were there at the highpoint just in case something went wrong, and stupid me; I had the flash on. Mike and I froze and stared at the house for several seconds to see if we were noticed. There was no movement, so we were still good.

Luckily, right before this trip, another Highpointers Club member submitted a hand-drawn map showing an alternate 'top secret' route to the highpoint. Instead of crossing through the madman's land, he detailed a way to walk around the entire perimeter of his property to gain access. I estimated his parcel to be approximately 2½-acres, so we decided to go this route to avoid any conflicts. Mike had the new map in-hand and started walking down the road.

"Hey! Where are you going? What do the directions say?" I whispered to Mike.

"What? Why are you talking so low?" he said aloud.

"Shhhhhh!" I ducked down and looked back towards the house. Then I said in an even higher whisper, "Because we are standing next to our car, next to this guy's house! Try to be a little quieter!"

"Stop shouting at me," Mike quietly said with a smile. He looked down at the map and read aloud, "Go eighty yards east of the driveway to an old abandoned jeep trail blocked with an old log and some barbed wire".

We found it almost immediately, and crossed the makeshift barricade onto his property. We were in and there was no turning back now. We assumed the log and fence were placed there to block this route as well. A lot of good that did.

"What next?" I whispered.

"Go 205 yards straight south into the woods to a fork in the trail".

"Trail? What trail?" I asked.

There was no trail, just a lot of thick brush under a lot of tall trees. We walked as straight south as we could through the brush trying to count out the 205 yards, and we did eventually find an obvious fork just as a faint trail emerged.

"Now what?" I whispered.

"It says to go about 273 yards west until we find a one foot high by three to four foot diameter white rock protruding onto the trail."

The trail was a little better at this point, but was still very overgrown. We came upon a rock that was similar to what was described in the directions. "What do you think Mike? Is this the rock? It seems as if we only went about 150 yards."

"Well, it says here that there is a faint trail leading off to the right from the rock."

We looked around and didn't see anything. "There's no trail here," I said. "I don't think we walked far enough yet. Let's keep going and see if we find another big rock like this one."

We kept going, but the trail fizzled down into practically nothing. We had to bushwhack through the thick foliage to get anywhere. Mike was wearing shorts, and his legs were getting pretty torn-up by all the thorns and branches. I always kept the madman's house in sight, which was off to the right of us at all times. We eventually came to another rock just like the first one.

"This must be it!" Mike said loudly, "This must be the one!"

"Shhhhhh!"

231

Right at that moment, we heard three gun shots out in the distance back from where we had just came from, "POP! POP! POP!" We both jumped and turned to the direction of the shots, then ducked down real low. It literally made the hair on the back of my neck stand up. I went from a little anxious to totally frightened at this point. I could picture this guy out there somewhere in the woods shooting into the air, trying to scare us; which was totally working by the way. We were deep on the backside of his property, and his house stood between us and the freedom of our getaway car. We sat there for a few minutes in total silence waiting to see if we heard anything coming towards us.

"Mike, let's get the hell out of here!"

"No way! We're almost there!" He whispered loudly

"What about the gun shots?" I asked with a lot of concern. "This isn't worth dying over." Just then there were a few more shots fired, "POP! POP! POP!" We sat there and stared through the trees, but didn't see or hear anything else for several minutes. These shots seemed to be a bit further away from us than the previous ones, so our concern did wane a little. "He must be looking for us in the other direction," I added, "OK then. We gotta do this one quickly, let's keep going. Where do we go from here?"

"It says there is a faint trail leading off to the right" Mike replied, "But there is no trail leading off anywhere." There wasn't even a trail leading from the first white rock we found to this one. We tromped around through thick brush for a few minutes, and couldn't find anything. We quietly went back to the first white rock to look around as well, and then went back to the second one again. It was a little creepy when we walked back to the first rock due to the fact that we were also walking back towards the guy with the gun.

"What else does it say Mike? Does it give any other clues?"

"It says to take the faint trail from the rock for 45 yards north until we find a shed-type building. The highpoint is right by the building somewhere next to a large tree marked with a big white "X".

I thought about it for a minute while Mike was still looking around, and then said. "OK, I think this is the rock. Let's go through the brush and look for the building." Mike agreed and we started north through the thick foliage. We had to crawl on our hands and knees under and through the thick undergrowth while keeping a lookout for the building. There was no way to tell which way we were going, and no telling what we would find.

"THERE IT IS!" Mike shouted.

"SHHHHHhhhh! Are you trying to get us caught? What the hell?!"

Then Mike whispered with a big smile, "There it is! I see the building".

"I know what you said you idiot! Hell, the guy shooting at us heard what you said as well! Keep it down." We crept towards the building that was just an old wooden shed with a metal roof, and then I saw the highpoint just across from it.

"There it is Mike!"

"SHHHHHHhhhh!"

Next to the tree was a big, flat, white rock that was definitely the highpoint. Even though we had to go all the way around this guy's property, the highpoint was right behind his house. We quickly whipped out our cameras and took our photos. They didn't come out well, so we turned on our flashes and retook them. I can't believe how stupid we were.

It was now time to get the hell out of there by going back the same way we came. Mike suggested that we just sneak past his house and go down his driveway. I wasn't going to have any part of that insanity; hell no. So we started back the way we came staying very quiet the whole time. I turned on my video camera and taped us all the way back to the car just in case we had any conflicts. I watched the tape several years later and could hear myself snickering at times. We walked the entire way (both ways) ducking and watching the house. I was also watching to see if this guy was ready to pounce on us from behind a tree somewhere as well. On the way back I realized we were both wearing bright white T-shirts. We might as well have been wearing cow bells around our necks as well. What a sense of relief it was when we finally made it back to the car. We had accomplished what most other highpointers avoided. We jumped into the car, honked our horn a couple of times to say thanks for the visit, then it was off on the next leg of our trip to Maine's breathtaking highpoint.

One thing was for certain: I never wanted to go through something like that again. No more hiking on private property for me. Nope! Never again.

Maine Katahdin
5,267' June 29, 1997

It took us all night to get from Jerimoth Hill in Rhode Island to Maine's highest mountain. I drove to the Massachusetts/New Hampshire state line, and then Mike got us the rest of the way to Katahdin while I slept. We planned this out perfectly and arrived on time early in the morning. This was necessary because the park opened daily at 6:00AM and operated on a "First come first served" basis. Only a limited number of cars were allowed in the park at any given time and we didn't... we couldn't miss our only opportunity at this mountain.

Mike planned on letting me sleep the whole night through, but woke me up when he got to a point where the entire road was blocked by a fallen tree. This was the only road leading into the park and there was nobody else there but us, so we figured we were the first to arrive. The tree was too big for us to do anything about, so we found a turn-out and parked the car so we could get about an hour's worth of sleep. We awoke at about 6:45AM as a convoy of cars was passing by on their way into the park. Mike started the car, jammed it into gear, and got our butts to the entrance gate in one hell of a hurry. We were 45 minutes late. Somebody had cleared the fallen tree while we slept, and we were very lucky we woke up in time to be among the first visitors in the park. We were a little worried that we may have missed our opportunity to get in, but luck was on our side and we had no issues.

We saw Katahdin through the trees as we drove towards the trail-head. What a formidable looking mountain it was. It stood nearly a mile high above the surrounding countryside, and was the only mountain out in that part of the country. It was huge.

"Oh my god, we have to go up that thing?" I commented.

"Yep!" Mike said with a huge smile.

We parked the car and started preparing for our four mile hike to the top. As I was getting ready, I suddenly realized that a silly childhood dream of mine had unexpectedly come true sometime in the middle of the night while I was sleeping. The moment Mike drove us over the border from New Hampshire into Maine, I had officially been in all fifty states. I thought about it for a few seconds to make sure, and sure enough it was true. I had always dreamed of visiting every state in the fifty United States ever since I was a child. It was another one of those lofty dreams I had as a kid, that I never really expected to become a reality.

"Mike, how many states have you been to?" I asked excitedly.

"I don't know. I guess all of them except for Alaska."

"Well, as of today, I have now been in all fifty states, including Alaska."

"You didn't climb Denali."

"I didn't say I climbed Denali. I said I have now been in all fifty states. I went to Alaska as a kid with my parents. Wow…"

"What?"

"I never really thought about it; that highpointing would allow me to visit all fifty states. I remember telling my dad when I was a kid that I wanted to see all fifty states one day, and now here I am! Done!"

"That's pretty cool."

"Yep!"

We gathered up what we needed and hit the trail; and what a trail it was. The first mile was good, and the last mile was good. It was the two miles in-between that were something else. Our guidebook had the hike listed as a class-1 hike. No way. I herby changed it to a class-3 climb. No doubt about it. It was two miles of going up approximately three thousand feet of elevation. It was hand holds and boulder hopping the whole way. At some points, we had to stop and figure out which was the better way to go: Up the cliffs, through the cracks, or up the smooth, slippery boulders the size of city buses. The trail was also just like Connecticut's; straight up. What was with those trail builders out there on the East Coast?

All the way up this two mile 'march of death', we kept hearing somebody up ahead of us howling: "AWOOOOOoooooooooooooo!" We heard this about every ten or fifteen minutes. Mike and I laughed every time we heard it. Somebody was definitely having a good time up there somewhere. We came across a natural spring gushing out of a golf ball sized hole in a rock. It was so bizarre. We took advantage of it to fill our canteens and to cool off a little. Again we heard the ever familiar, "AWOOOOOoooooooooooooo!" while we were resting there. I tried in haste to answer the call, but my voice does not carry well and I don't think they ever heard it.

When we finally made it to the ridge, the topography totally leveled-off and we could see the peak out in the distance with several people milling around on it. As I walked that last mile, we heard the ever familiar, "AWOOOOOoooooooooooooo!" coming from that same direction. I couldn't wait to see who it was that had kept us entertained for the last few hours. As for the terrain, there were no trees or bushes up there; just grass and rock. We were above the timber line at about 3500 feet, which was strange to me because the timberline I was used too, like that found on the western highpoints like Mount Whitney and Boundary Peak, was at 11,500 feet. I could only assume that this was due to the fact that we were much more north than any of those in the west that I had hiked. The 360 degree view was spectacular. Trees and lakes as far as the eye could see. Green, green, green.

We met a lot of people up there. There was this one bunch in particular who I will never forget. I affectionately called them, "The Crazy Canadians." There were eight of them, and they were a blast. As soon as they found out we were from Los Angeles, they let us have it with all the O.J. jokes, gangs, smog, traffic, etc. We already knew how bad it was and didn't need to be reminded. As Mike and I were taking some pictures, a woman right next to me let out the very familiar, "AWOOOOOoooooooooooooo!" It was the Crazy Canadians!

We ended up hiking back down the mountain with them, and talked about important topics, like 'beer'. All they did on the way down was tell jokes (mainly at Mike's and my expense), and beer. They were a blast. They made it very pleasurable for the hike back down. "What kind of beer do you like" I asked.

"Beer" they shot back. This one lady with them was somewhat afraid of heights, and literally slid on her butt for those two miles of tough trail. At one point she said in her beautiful accent, "I'm goin' t' git a hole n da seat of me ass." One of the others replied, "Just keep in mind a flat of beer is waiting for us in the car, mate." With that, they all smiled and continued on with a little more motivation. She sounded like she had an Irish accent more than a Canadian one, so I asked where her accent was from. She replied in a very snotty tone, "I don't have the accent… you do!" and that was the end of that conversation.

When we finally made it back to the cars, and it turned out that we were all parked right next to each other. They offered us a beer (Budweiser), and we all socialized a little more before we went our separate ways. I sure wish I would have got their names and numbers. I would have definitely 'hooked-up' with them if I ever went back up to that part of the country again. We invited them to join us on our next highpoint in New Hampshire, but they declined stating that they needed to get more American beer and get back across the border to Canada before it closed for the night.

Before we departed, Mike asked if anybody knew how Canada got its name. Nobody knew, so Mike went on to explain, "When the first two settlers, Jacques and Pierre, arrived in the Great White North, they had no idea what to name it. Jacques had a great idea and proceeded to write down every letter of the alphabet on individual strips of parchment. He then placed them into his hat and told Pierre to pull three letters out one at a time and say what each letter was. Jacques would then write down these letters as they were called out to see what great name for their new land they could come up with.

Pierre pulled the first letter out of the hat and said, "C, eh"!
Jacques wrote <u>CA</u>.

Pierre pulled the second letter out of the hat and said, "N, eh"!

Jacques wrote <u>NA</u>.

Pierre then pulled the third and final letter out of the hat and said, "D, eh"!

Jacques wrote <u>DA</u>.

Pierre got all excited and asked, "Well? What do we have?"

Jacques raised his hands high up in the air and shouted, "CANADA!"

…Yeah, the joke fell pretty flat with our new Canadian friends as well. "AWOOOOOoooooooooooooo!"

New Hampshire Mount Washington
6,288' June 30, 1997

This was our final peak of the "Logistical Nightmare." This was also going to be my fortieth peak overall. I would now qualify for the 40 Peak Pin just like the one I awarded Mike back in New Jersey. I couldn't wait until the next day when I would basically award it to myself. We arrived at the entrance well after closing time, so I parked the car nearby in a field. I turned off the motor, reclined my seat, and covered up for the night. I thought that Mike was sleeping the whole time, but I heard him softly chuckling to himself.

"What?" I asked.

"This is awesome…"

"What?"

"Here we are again out in the middle of nowhere thousands of miles away from home sleeping in a car."

I laughed and looked over at Mike who was also all covered up for the night. "Mike," I said, "There is nobody else on the planet that would have done this with me. Thanks." I reached out my hand, we shook, and then we were both out for the night.

The next morning we paid the entrance fee and made our way to the top. I think it was about ten miles from the gate. The peak was mainly just a tourist attraction, and there was a visitor's center and weather station up there. We found the actual highpoint and took our photos. You cannot tell by the pictures, but there were buildings and people all around the highpoint. We took the photos at special angles to make it look as if it was just us and the mountain. After I jumped off the peak (about a three foot high rock), I whipped out my 40 Peak Pin and proudly pinned it to my Jacket. This pin was very hard earned, and I wanted it displayed for all to see... even if nobody else with the exception of Mike knew what it was. Mike congratulated me with a highpoint hug and said, "We're almost there."

While Mike walked around taking photos, I stood there at the summit and thought to myself what a huge accomplishment this was. I now had forty peaks completed with only eight more to go. Damn I had come such a long way. I could feel the excitement gushing throughout my entire body. I couldn't wait to get the remaining eight mountains. I was so close now. Doing this climb also meant that the entire eastern half of the United States was now complete for me. What an awesome day that was. Now I just had to finish off the western half where my remaining eight peaks awaited.

Besides being the highest point in New Hampshire, this peak also had another claim to fame: It was also the windiest spot on earth. Winds in excess of two hundred miles per hour were clocked there regularly, with the average daily wind speed being seventy miles per hour. We were very lucky that day as the winds were only blowing at about twenty miles per hour. They actually have a building up there that is chained to the ground to prevent it from blowing away! After we took our pictures, we had four hours to get back to Boston to catch the last flight out to Los Angeles. We returned the rental car with an additional 2293 miles on it, caught the flight with time to spare, and it was off to home again.

On top of New Hampshire with my 40 Peak Pin

The next trip I had planned would be in two months where I would be climbing Wheeler Peak, New Mexico, and Harney Peak, South Dakota. These were the two peaks I passed up on two previous trips. Mike being the amazing person he always was wanted to come along again which was totally awesome. I didn't want to do them alone, and who better to have with you during hikes like these? One thing was for certain, I was going to get them this time. Mike actually made me promise this which I did whole-heartedly.

Chapter 12
- Third Time's A Charm

While planning for this trip, our hiking buddy Joe decided that he wanted to come along for the ride. He was an avid hiker and wanted to see what this highpointing stuff was all about. He said he wanted to get to some peaks that he would otherwise never really have a chance to climb, and this was his golden opportunity. We warned him repeatedly of what he was to expect on this trip; driving, hiking, driving, hiking, and, well... driving. He didn't seem to have a problem with that, so he was in. We had everything pretty much planned and we would soon be off to get the two I missed... twice.

New Mexico Wheeler Peak
13,161' August 15, 1997

Anna stopped me as I was walking out the front door and made me promise to get these two mountains this time. Travelling all of that distance to only come back empty handed was not going to be acceptable for a third time. I promised her that I would, and she said not to come home unless I did.

"Well, what if I don't?" I jokingly asked.

"Then don't come home until you do."

"Deal!"

After a long hug and kiss, I went out front and found Mike and Joe waiting for me in yet another rental car; they had come to my house together to pick me up since I was 'on the way'. I threw my backpack into the trunk and jumped into the back seat. We were off on another adventure that would take us thousands of miles and ultimately net me two more highpoints. We were only a couple minutes into our drive when Mike suggested that we stop in Laughlin on the way to throw some dice; this idea was immediately agreed to by all. About an hour later while driving through the sweltering Mojave Desert, Mike was caught speeding and received the one and only speeding ticket we ever received during our entire highpointing experience. We had been pretty lucky to that point; there was no doubt about that. It was bound to happen sooner or later, I was just glad it didn't happen to me. While in Laughlin, I blew away $20.00 in nickels in about thirty minutes and decided that it just wasn't my day... again. I had been having bad luck in Vegas and Laughlin for many years and always knew when to call it quits. I gathered up the boys, and we were back on the road with no delay. We needed to get to Wheeler as soon as we possibly could so we would have enough time to get some descent sleep and start our hike early the next morning.

As we approached Flagstaff, Arizona, Joe stated that he was getting hungry. "No problem," Mike said, "There's gotta be a Subway in Flagstaff somewhere."

"Subway?" Joe hungrily responded, "I love Subway!"

"I guess Joe's in the club!" I shot back.

"How's it goin' eh!?"

We found one located in a gas station, and that was Joe's first introduction to one of our many highpointing traditions. He had already been somewhat introduced to the tradition a week prior when we all hiked San Jacinto Peak overlooking Palm Springs in Southern California. We hiked this 10,834 foot peak in preparation for Wheeler Peak. When we got to the top, Mike pulled a small Igloo cooler from his backpack and produced a couple Subway sandwiches. That was a huge and welcome surprise to both Joe and I.

After the seven hour drive from Flagstaff, we finally arrived at the Wheeler Peak trailhead at about 3:00AM. Mike found us a place to park, and we immediately settled in for a few hours of sleep in the car. Mike brought along an alarm clock; the kind with the two bells mounted on the top. He placed it on the dashboard after he set it to wake us in the morning. When that thing went off a few hours later, I jumped up in my seat and almost hit my head on the roof of the car. Talk about a heart attack. Joe was just as shocked and shouted, "What the hell is that?!" Mike was rubbing his eyes and laughing as he slowly reached out and turned it off and said, "Loud, huh?!"

We wanted to start the hike at 6:00AM, but we totally forgot about the one hour time difference now that we were in the next time zone. I realized this when I looked at my watch just as we started the hike and noticed it was 7:00AM. An hour could mean a lot up there and our largest concern were the monsoons which usually occurred in that part of the country in the late afternoons. We needed to get off the mountain by 3:00PM at the latest. This was also my first hike above thirteen thousand feet since Colorado several years prior, and I was feeling a little bit apprehensive about it. As a matter of fact, the highest mountain I had been on since Colorado was Guadalupe Peak in Texas which stood at only 8,749 feet. So, not only was I going above thirteen thousand feet for the first time in many years, but this was also pretty darn lofty for someone like me who didn't often go up that high. I was only concerned because I was not in as good of shape as I had been on my previous climbs. But on the flipside, I did have a strong mindset and I knew that I was going to be standing on top of New Mexico by lunchtime. I had a promise to keep with both Mike and Anna as well as with myself, and I was not prepared to let any of us down.

It was a great trail and we all kicked some serious butt that day. Mike had brought along this huge hiking stick that he fashioned out of a small tree or something. He looked like Moses walking the trail with this thing, and he got several comments about it during our hike. About halfway to the top, he got tired of carrying it and stashed it somewhere alongside the trail. "I hope nobody steals it", he said.

"I hope you remember where you hid it on the way back down", I replied.

"Me too."

248

The weather was perfect all of the way to the top, and I was really lucky that this hike turned out to be a piece of cake. We went above the timber line about two-thirds the way to the top. Once out from under the cool tree cover, I found the sun to be very strong and I got pretty sunburned by the time the day was over. There was a little bit of snow here and there, but we didn't have to walk through any. There was one spot on the trail near the top that was so windy, I could lean into it and wouldn't fall. That was pretty cool. If the wind had abruptly stopped, I would have fallen flat on my face and tumbled back down the trail.

On top of New Mexico with my 30 Peak Pin

There were a few people at the top when we arrived, as well as a couple guys from Texas who were up there on horseback. That was the first time I had ever seen horses up so high. The only other time would be in Utah the following year during my 'shocking' Kings Peak odyssey. The view was fantastic, and I could see way out into the pink and orange New Mexico desert in all directions. At that point, I now qualified for the 30 Peak Pin; the same pin I awarded Mike back in New York. I was so excited about finally reaching the summit of Wheeler that I had totally forgotten all about the pin until I got to South Dakota later the next day. My next award (and my last) would be the 48 Peak Plaque which I was really looking forward to receiving one day in the near future. That plaque was as good as mine and they might as well had started getting it ready for me as far as I was concerned.

Joe, me and Mike on top of New Mexico

I could not believe that I was finally standing on top of Wheeler Peak. I was not able to do it during my Mid-west Extravagonzo due to Ron's foot problems, and I was not able to attempt it during our trip to get the ones we missed due to the crazy weather as well as the issues I was experiencing with my ankle and knee. All that didn't matter any longer since I was now triumphantly standing on top of New Mexico! What a feeling that was. I turned to Mike and gave him one of his own highpoint hugs. I then thanked him for being such a pal and coming with me on the trip. His response was, "It ain't over yet! You still gotta get Harney tomorrow".

"Not a problem!" I enthusiastically responded.

I then turned to Joe and said, "Come here. I've got a highpoint hug waiting for you too."

"What the hell is a highpoint hug?"

I gave him one, then Mike gave him one, then Joe said, "I just drove halfway across the country and climbed the highest mountain in New Mexico with a couple of fruit loops."

We all laughed pretty hard over that one.

We found a place to sit and have a small lunch before our descent. The trail getting to the top was six miles in length, but by studying the maps beforehand, I knew of a short cut back down to the car that would shave off a couple miles and about an hour. There was no trail on this alternate route, and it was extremely steep. It didn't take much to talk the guys into doing it, and it would get us to South Dakota that much quicker. The first mile was just like coming off Nevada's highpoint; practically running and jumping down the entire way through the gravel. That was one of the fastest miles I had ever done. The slope was probably like sixty degrees for most of the way. When I got down to more level terrain, I started noticing the weakness in my legs. It took so much energy coming down that first mile that my legs were becoming like rubber bands. Every once and a while I would step wrong, and my legs would go out from under me just from shear weakness alone. I had to sit down quite often to give my legs a break. This was due to me being out of shape, but it didn't really matter at this point because I had conquered Wheeler, and the next day's climb in South Dakota wouldn't be so demanding.

The last two miles back down to the car were a killer. While I was coming down that first mile up top, I was unknowingly jamming my big toes into the front of my boots. I didn't notice this until I started lagging way behind the others because one of my toes was hurting so badly. The last mile was the worst and I was really in a lot of pain. Even though I was suffering a little, I was totally relieved and lucky it wasn't my stupid knee this time.

I did end up losing a toenail off my right foot a month later because of that. This shortcut did save us some time, but it was brutal. Would I ever take it again? Probably. As we were driving away from the mountain, I reminded Mike about his hiking stick he left up on the mountain.

"Damn! Looks like I'll have to find another one!"

A little more info on our friend Joe: He was a skinny, lanky, retired gentleman with grey hair who was an avid hiker and mountain climber. One thing I learned about this man was not to let his outward appearance fool you. He did not look it, but he was always able to kick some serious butt during our mountain climbs, and on many occasions made *me* feel old. Mike and Joe had been friends for years before we were introduced, and just like Mike, he had a funny yet strange sense of humor which allowed him to fit right in with us. He was actually on my Mount Hood trip back in 1994, and was the guy who came back to the hut with me that night I gave up. He was also one of the people who made it to the top the very next day while I was travelling home. He had also completed Mount Whitney a few times just like me. Wheeler Peak was his third highpoint, and he wasn't even a highpointer. Mike and I secretly planned a little something for him after he completed Harney Peak the next day, but in order for that to happen, we needed to make an undisclosed detour in Nebraska.

South Dakota Harney Peak Attempt # 2
7,242' August 16, 1997

Panorama Point in Nebraska was basically on the way to South Dakota, so we took the thirty mile detour so Joe could unknowingly get his fourth highpoint. Mike and I both persuaded him into wanting to go to Nebraska's highpoint, but he did not have any idea what Mike and I were up to. That information would not come to light until the next morning on top of South Dakota. We arrived on Panorama Point about 11:00PM on August 15, 1997. Joe thought it was pretty cool that a highpoint could be out in the middle of the Great Plains with no real mountain in sight. This was of course mine and Mike's second visit to this highpoint. Since we were there, we also took him to the tri-state marker located nearby and shared our Subway picnic story with him. Now all we had to do was to drive all night to our next destination in South Dakota.

It was my shift to drive, and I had us headed north to South Dakota in no time. I came down with a bad cold somewhere in the heart of Nebraska, and it hit me pretty hard and fast. I pulled into a tiny all night convenience store in some small, podunk town with a population of about 47 people and ten thousand cows. I bought some cold medicine, and it was lights out for me the rest of the way to Harney. Either Mike or Joe got us the rest

253

of the way there… I don't recall. I just needed this rest so I could get my butt to the top of South Dakota the next morning. Nothing was going to stop me. I could not break my promise to Mike or Anna, and most of all to myself.

Joe's fourth highpoint

Mike got us to the trailhead at about 6:00AM. We immediately started our hike, and all made it to the top by about 8:30AM. On the way up, we came upon a very tall tree that had only partially fallen because it got stuck on another tree's branches on the way down. Mike never liked to see things half done, so he jumped at the opportunity to complete the process. He got those two trees swaying back and forth, until the fallen tree finally broke loose and came crashing down to the forest floor… totally blocking the trail. We all stood there staring in silence at what Mike had done, and then he said, "I gave the mountain a little something to remember me by."

We continued up the trail about another half mile from that point to reach the summit. The top was a very beautiful place and simply magnificent how they built the rock observation tower to seem as if it was actually part of the mountain itself. It was the most beautifully taken care of peak out of all the peaks I had visited to date.

Once all three of us reached the top, we pulled Joe aside and awarded him with a Highpointers Club Five Peaks Patch, the same patch that Mike had awarded me back in Colorado some years prior. Joe was very surprised and happy that we did this for him. He couldn't stop talking about it; especially after we told him that it was the reason we had visited Nebraska's highpoint the night before so he would qualify.

Joe holding his award on his fifth highpoint

We also took a few minutes to award me with my 30 Peak Pin. This was the pin that I should have received back in New Mexico the day before. It was somewhat ironic to me that I would receive my 40 peak pin back in New Hampshire six weeks before my 30 Peak one... and this was my 42nd peak. Mike congratulated me on finally completing the two mountains that took me three attempts to accomplish, and I triumphantly responded with, "Third time's a charm!"

Because I knew that I would probably never get back to this part of the country. I took more time during the hike back down to the car to take in the beautiful scenery. I was really surprised at all the different rocks and things in the area. Huge boulders of pink quartz were sticking out of the ground, and there were these other rocks that were very shiny, and looked like silver. When I picked them up, they flaked apart in my hands. Some places on the trail were completely covered by these silver flakes. What a beautiful, wonderful place this was.

Now it was time to head on back home. What a long drive from South Dakota to Southern California that was. Mike mentioned his previous brief encounter with the cute girl as we passed the area she was working the last time we were there. "Keep your eyes open. Maybe she is still working up here somewhere." He said with wide eyes and a big smile.

"Don't get your hopes up Mike."

"How's it goin' eh!?"

The drive sure went a lot easier with three people. Mike and I got more rest than what we were accustomed to because of Joe, and we took advantage of it. I was sound asleep in the passenger seat while we were driving south somewhere through Utah when I was suddenly awakened by an immediate, horrendous headache. It was absolutely terrible and felt as if my head was going to explode. The pain was everywhere: all around my scalp, in my eyes, my ears, my teeth, everywhere. It actually brought tears to my eyes and I could not find any relief. I asked Mike for something to help kill the pain, and he produced some Tylenol, or Excedrin, or something. I remember swallowing five or six of whatever he gave me and it started working within minutes. I had experienced this exact type of headache once before when it awakened me from my sleep at home in bed about a year prior to this event. I don't know what kind of headache that was, maybe a migraine? After experiencing something so dreadful, I felt so sorry for people who suffered from this on a regular basis. I always thought that this was some sort of after affect from my bout with Meningitis a few years prior. I have never experienced it since and hope it stays that way. It was all better by the time we stopped in Vegas to throw some dice, play some blackjack and slots... and oh yeah; enjoy the all you can eat pancakes for .99 cents.

I now had 42 highpoints completed, and Mike had 44 (including Hawaii, Oregon and Washington). I thought back to when I stood on Humphreys Peak in Arizona and only had one highpoint completed, and 48 seemed and was so far away. But now with only a few left to go, I could see the light at the end of the tunnel. Mike and I had 'cranked-out' 36 highpoints in three years which was in itself an amazing feat. I knew it wouldn't be like that from that point on though. The remaining mountains were going to be really tough. I also needed to catch up with

Mike a bit. He had Mount Hood, Oregon, and Mount Rainier, Washington under his belt, and I needed both of those to catch up with him. That next year in 1998, I planned on completing them both in one single trip. I also planned on completing Kings Peak, Utah in September of that same year. After that, it would be one peak a year for the three following years until they were all completed. I had a solid plan, and I knew in my heart that there was nothing *foreseeable* that could
stop me…

Chapter 13
- Catch Up Time

Not only did I need Mount Hood, Oregon, and Mount Rainier, Washington to get me that much closer to my goal, but like I said previously, I needed them to catch up with Mike as well. Once I had these two mountains conquered, Mike and I would finally be equals in our mountain climbing quest. I didn't want him to get too far ahead of me because I had always planned on us capturing our 48th mountain together. I last attempted Mount Hood four years prior in 1994 and had failed miserably. Now, I was in top physical health, shape, and in the right frame of mind. The only way that I would not get this mountain is if the mountain itself had just disappeared.

This trip was designed so that we would climb Mount Hood in one day, drive to Mount Rainier the next, then spend two days on that mountain; capturing it on the second day. I spent months planning for this trip, and decided at the last minute to open it up to the company's hiking club. Once I did this, I had a flurry of applicants and ended up with eight dedicated people: John H., Jeff S., Ted W., Mike K., James B., Kelly A., Joe S., and myself. We were all very motivated and ready. Mike Gauthier was initially going to do these two mountains with me, but backed out just weeks before the main event due to prior commitments. Since he was not going to be joining us, I borrowed his hi-tech plastic snow boots and crampons so I wouldn't have the same ridiculous issues I had during my previous attempt.

Jeff S. was a seasoned mountain climber, so I designated him the leader of the climb itself; while I would lead all of the logistics of getting there, hotels, cars, etc. Jeff took us up in the San Bernardino Mountains during the winter of 1998 for some mountaineering training. He educated us on walking in the snow with crampons, rope training, arresting falls, and many other aspects of snow and ice climbing. He also arranged to have a friend of his, another seasoned mountain climber, train us on rope care and handling, as well as how to tie the proper knots, how to climb out of crevasses, and everything else we were going to need to be successful up there. And as an added bonus, he had also climbed both of these mountains, and gave us all sorts of tips on where the main crevasses were, where to take breaks, where ropes were required, where not to go, etc. This information was invaluable and we were sure lucky to have him.

One thing I will never forget about the training was how to arrest a fall. He trained us how to stop ourselves from sliding down a mountain uncontrollably. He had us practice sliding on our stomachs faced down the hill, and then faced up the hill. He then trained us on our backs faced uphill, and then faced downhill. This last one was tough and a little scary. It was also the hardest one to stop. I ripped a large hole in my brand-new waterproof pants with my ice axe while practicing this one, but was still able to stop myself successfully. This one guy slid the whole way down and ended up in the bushes way below. It was fun, but also very serious. These were matters of life and death we were learning here. Mount Hood was the second most climbed mountain in the world, only after Mount Fuji in Japan. The climb is attempted by about ten thousand people a year. Because of these factoids, people always assumed that it was really easy to accomplish. When I thought about the 130 people who had died attempting to climb Mount Hood, I began to realize just how serious this all was.

Oregon Mount Hood Attempt # 2
11,239' June 12, 1998

We were all to meet at LAX in the morning to catch our flight to Portland. Who knew it was going to rain that day. For those who are not familiar with Interstate 405 in Southern California, it turns into a parking lot on rainy days because people here don't know how to drive in the rain. James and I got to the airport about twenty minutes after our plane had departed. I also had Mike K's ticket with me and wondered if he had got on the plane with the others or not. As soon as we walked into the ticketing area, there he was waiting for us.

I was able to change our flight to the very next one, and we spent the next few hours having beers for breakfast in the airport lounge. I was a little concerned about the other five people because they didn't know which rental car agency to go to in Portland. I was supposed to be there with them to take care of this stuff. I was really worried and hoping that they would all be OK. We eventually got on our flight and were finally on our way. We were about three hours behind the others and they were probably already there trying to figure things out. There was nothing I could do, so I tried to get some sleep.

During the flight, one of the strangest things to ever happen to me occurred. When I was sleeping on the plane, a huge wave of fear swept over my entire body which woke me instantly. I ended up sitting upright in my seat scared out of my wits looking around me for no apparent reason at all. I was short of breath and my heart was racing. Why was I experiencing this extreme anxiety? I am usually a little scared to fly, but it wasn't that at all. I was really frightened and I couldn't figure out why. I looked at my watch and it was about 1:40PM. I looked around and nobody noticed what I was doing. I was glad about this because it would have been a little embarrassing. I sat back in my seat and tried to relax, but the feeling of fear just wouldn't go away. I just tried to relax the best I could until I was able to finally shake it off.

We landed in Portland where I immediately started looking for the others as soon as we got off the plane; they were nowhere in sight. We retrieved our baggage and they were not there either. We went outside to get a ride to the car rental agency and they were not there as well. When we got to Alamo, I asked if they had been there, and they had. This was great news. Jeff knew where the hotel was where we were spending that night, so I guessed that he must have taken everybody up there already. We got our car and headed up to the mountain to meet the others. As soon as we got to the hotel, we found everybody there safe and sound. As it turned out, they did have a hard time determining which rental car agency I used, but after they figured it out everything else fell into place. We all went out to dinner and discussed the events of the day as well as our pending climb.

When we got back to the hotel, I learned that it was a requirement to carry avalanche transmitters when climbing Mount Hood. The way these things worked was that if we were caught in an avalanche, a member of the team was to simply pull a pin and alarms would sound everywhere to alert emergency workers to come to the rescue. There were receivers set up all over the mountain to monitor for these signals if a transmitter was to ever go off. One avalanche transmitter was required per rope team, and since there were eight of us, we decided on two rope teams of four people each. I was elected to carry the transmitter for my team, and Jeff would carry the other for his. We wore them around our neck and under our arms like a bandolier so that if we were caught in an avalanche, they would not come off very easily and give us plenty of time to pull those pins.

I went by myself to the hotel lobby to rent the transmitters. During some small talk with the clerk, I had mentioned that I was not only going to do Mount Hood, but also Mount Rainier in a few days as well. The man's jaw dropped, and he had a huge look of concern on his face.

"What's wrong?" I asked.

"Haven't you been listening to the news today?" he replied.

"No… Why?"

He turned around and turned on the TV above his desk. There on the screen was live news coverage of a rescue occurring up on Mount Rainier. Two rope teams had been caught in an avalanche. Many were seriously hurt and one man had died. One of the rope teams had slid off of a cliff, while the other clung onto the cliff face. Some were dangling from one rope which was frayed to the inner strands while pulled tight over a sharp rock. The team that went over the cliff was also able to hold on somehow while keeping one man who was dangling at the end of the rope from falling three hundred feet to the glacier below. When the rescuers were finally able to lower this man to safety, he had already died from exposure.

I stood there and watched all of this in total disbelief. This little bit of reality gave me a huge slap in the face. This wasn't all fun and games anymore; this was now very real and very serious. As I watched, I heard the announcer say that the avalanche had occurred at approximately 1:40 that afternoon. My mind went blank for a moment… this was the same exact time that I had had my episode on the plane. I experienced many emotions at that exact moment, and the same fear that had awakened me during my flight was now coursing through me like a locomotive. I became short of breath again, and my heart started to race. I felt slight pressure on my chest and I started to tear-up a little. It was at that instant that I decided I would not be climbing Mount Rainier on this trip. I didn't hesitate in this decision, not even for a second. What made matters worse for me was the fact that the avalanche occurred on the same route we were going to be taking.

I walked up to our room and told everybody of the news. Somebody turned on the television and everybody stood and stared in disbelief. They were all silent as they huddled around to watch. After a few minutes, I made my announcement that I would do Hood, but would not be doing Rainier. As soon as I said this, John H. and James also said that they would not be climbing Rainier either as this was just too much to deal with. This upset the others, but it didn't matter. My safety was my number one priority, and I didn't want to risk it by climbing some stupid mountain.

As we continually monitored the news, we learned that the climbers on Rainer were all from Southern California. Not only that, but they were all from the same cities as we were. I immediately called my mom who was absolutely freaking out. After I calmed her down I told her of my decision not to climb Rainier. She made me promise that I would keep my word, and I assured her that I would. I then called Anna who luckily didn't know anything about what had happened and was very happy with my decision and glad that I would be coming home a couple days early. I then called my work where many of my friends and colleagues who had heard the news were also very concerned and upset as well.

I had rented us a huge room large enough for all eight of us, and we all settled in for the night. I had a very hard time sleeping that night as my mind was racing at a million miles an hour. The avalanche on Rainier was strong on my mind, but what was even more on my mind was the fact that I had previously failed to climb *this* mountain. What if I failed again? I didn't want to fail, and I didn't think I was going to fail, but what if I did? I didn't want to be unsuccessful a second time. I told myself over and over that I was 100% ready for this mountain, and there was no way I wasn't going to get to the top. I was physically and mentally ready.

We all awoke at 1:00AM to start getting ready for our 2:30AM start. You have to climb this mountain in the middle of the night while the snow is frozen solid. As the sun rises, the snow turns to slush which makes it near impossible to climb. All of our backpacks weighed-in at about 25 pounds each, but James' weighed in at an unreasonable 45 pounds. I asked him what he had in there and told him to get rid of everything that wouldn't be required for the climb. He refused to take anything out which I still think to this day was a huge part of his downfall later during the climb.

We drove ourselves up to the trailhead and found the register to sign. Signing the register was required so that people would know who was up on the mountain at any given time. We were also informed that just twelve days prior on May 31, several people were caught by an avalanche on the same route we were taking. One person had died, and one had some very serious injuries. This occurred just above the Hog's Back where a large slab of snow and ice broke loose and swept the rope team of three down the mountain. The one that was killed was found under four feet of snow about an hour after the avalanche occurred.

Everybody looked at me, and I immediately responded that this news was not going to stop me from climbing this mountain. When I was asked why Rainier was so different, I could not answer. They didn't know what had happened to me on the flight, and I was not planning to share this information. I admit that I was a little embarrassed about it, but what happened just struck too much fear into me and I just knew in my heart that I would not be able to complete Rainier; not on this trip anyway. I asked them all to please not bug me about it anymore and to just let it go; which they did.

The mountain was fully lit by the moon and was just beautiful. Even though the peak was four miles away in the middle of the night, I could see it as if I were looking at it in the middle of the day. I planned this trip around the full moon for this very reason. The mountain starts off very gradual, but the further up the mountain you go, the steeper it gets. By the time you are near the top, it is very steep and that is where all of our training would eventually pay off.

Our first scheduled rest stop was about a mile up the mountain at the Silcox Hut; the same place I had stayed the last time I was on this mountain. It was kind of strange to see it again. It was all closed up and dark this time around, but it sure brought back some memories. The last time I was there, there was a blizzard occurring. This time it was calm and absolutely perfect. Several of us all arrived at the hut together, but there were a few stragglers. We waited as they all came in one at a time. James with his heavy backpack was the last to arrive about thirty minutes after I got there and was simply exhausted. The worst part about his situation was the fact that this first mile was the easiest. It got much tougher from this point on. I think James announced almost immediately that he was done. We all tried to talk him out of quitting, but his mind was made up. We tried to talk him into stashing some of his stuff to lighten his pack, but he wouldn't budge. I fully understood what he was going through both physically and mentally, so we let him go.

As for me, I was feeling great. The last time I was standing at this same exact spot, I was scared and anxiety ridden, there was a blizzard blowing, my crampons kept falling off, and I was just not prepared in any way, shape or form. Even though I only had about an hour of sleep this night, I was feeling 100% and wanted to keep going. Our next scheduled rest stop was another mile up the mountain where the ski lifts drop off the skiers during ski season. We all said our goodbyes to James and we were off. James would have no problem finding his way back to the cars as the parking lot and nearby hotel were fully lit and hard to miss.

Even though the mountain was getting a little steeper as we kept ourselves going higher, we all made very good time to the next stop. All of us made it pretty much together, except for John H. who was taking his time getting up there. It took him about thirty minutes to arrive after the last person. It turned out that he had severe blisters on his feet that were totally agonizing him to no end. He announced that he was done and we all let him go as well. It was two miles down to the car, and I felt sorry for him having to walk all that distance with his feet the way they were. Again, we didn't have any issue letting him walk back alone for the same reason as James.

That rest stop was also a very major milestone for me... huge. It was at this point on my previous attempt that I had quit and turned back. I took a very good look at myself at that moment and realized that I was a much different person now than I was back then. I was still at 100% and I was going to conquer this beast this time. I couldn't believe the motivation that was pumping through me. What an awesome feeling that was. This was going to be a huge win for me and I could already imagine myself standing on the top, arms held high in the air, with a big smile on my face.

The next scheduled break was at a place on the mountain called The Hog's Back. This is where we would all separate into teams and rope-up. Getting up there was tough. It was really starting to get steep and the morning sun was starting to rise. It was getting so tough that I just had to pace myself and get into a certain frame of mind: Step… step… breathe… Step… step… breathe… This was so important and got me most of the way to our next stop.

We were all climbing in a single-file line with Mike K. leading the way. This guy was an animal. He would climb way ahead of us as if it were nothing, and wait for us all to catch up. There were times when he, or even others, would accidentally knock large blocks of icy snow loose. People would yell out "LOOK OUT!" so we could avoid these missiles as they shot past us. There was another team or two up ahead of us, and every once in a while a huge snowball would come racing past us out of nowhere. They were breaking stuff loose just as we were. I wondered about the people down below us and what they were thinking.

When the sun started rising on the opposite side of the mountain from us, it cast a huge shadow of the mountain on the cloud tops that were way down below us at this point. I didn't realize how high up on the mountain we were until I took a look back. What an awesome sight it was.

Somehow along the way, I took over the lead and started up a very steep section of the mountain that would lead us up to The Hog's Back. I was still feeling very motivated and very good. This was really turning into a great day for me. The mountain was so steep at this point that I had to punch my ice axe into the snow up in front of me, then with my boots I had to create steps in the ice for the others to follow. I was not really paying attention as to how steep it really was until I knocked a block of snow loose. "LOOK OUT!" I shouted. I looked back to the others to make sure they were OK and they were not behind me at all. They were all straight down below me! When I say down, I mean down. From my angle, all I could see were the tops of their helmets. At that point I leaned into the cliff and froze-up for a minute (no pun intended). Kelly was down behind me and asked if I was OK. I told her that I didn't realize it was so steep and to give me a minute to figure things out. I looked up and I was leading us straight to a shear wall of solid ice that we would not be able to climb. I yelled down to everybody to start working their way towards the right where the steepness eventually gave way to a slightly gentler slope. After about five minutes of working myself towards the right as the others were also doing below me, I found myself standing on top of The Hog's Back by myself.

This was our third and final pit-stop before our final push to the summit. I took off my backpack, Put on my heavy coat, pulled out some snacks, and waited for the rest of the team to join me. I couldn't see any of them because they were so far below me. I sat down and gazed out across the beautiful views as I opened a bag of Peanut M&Ms. The bag was pressurized and looked like a small balloon. As soon as I opened the bag, it made a loud "Pop!" and every one of my M&Ms shot out of the bag and rolled down the mountain leaving little trails of rainbow colors behind them in the snow. I still couldn't see anybody yet, but I heard somebody down below say, "What the hell!?" And then I heard laughter from a couple others. It was pretty funny.

I sat there for about twenty minutes before the next person arrived. It was Kelly. I asked her where everybody else was and she pointed down. I looked and there they all were making their way up the same way I had come... the real steep way. I don't know why they decided on this, but it was no wonder why it was taking them so long. Once everybody made it, Joe walked up to me and said something I will never forget. He said: "John, you're an animal. I really didn't think that you would make it this far, but now I know you are going to make it all the way." Wow. I don't know why he had that impression about me, but his words took my motivation up to 1000%. I already knew that I was going to make it, but his words gave me that extra boost I needed.

We divided up into two rope-teams of three people each. There was some concern that we lost two people on the way up, and that we should have had four people per rope-team. We moved a couple people around until we were satisfied with the teams, then started working our way to the summit. We still had a long way to go, and there was no stopping us now. The first thing we had to do from here was to go around a huge crevasse. This thing was big enough to swallow a small house. The climb got extremely steep from this point on, and I was always at the ready if I or anybody on my rope were to slip and fall. If anybody fell, it was up to all three people on the rope to arrest the fall. I also always kept my hand near the pin on the avalanche transmitter. I was always at the ready if anything were to happen; I took this responsibility very serious.

As we were slowly working our way up, I noticed off to the left of us an enormous area of loose, broken-up snow and ice where the avalanche had just killed the climber just twelve days prior. I told the others on my rope team and we all stopped to look and soak it in. I said that this was not going to happen to us and we all continued on our way. It was a little sad and eerie being there, but this event kept me on my guard for the rest of the climb.

Because the sun was up and it was about 10:00AM, the ice all around us started cracking. It sounded spooky as it popped and creaked, and I could just imagine a huge chunk of ice breaking off and carrying us down the mountain like what had happened to those poor hikers. We also had to climb beneath some cliffs where little pieces of ice were falling off and creating snowballs that got bigger and bigger the further down the mountain they got, just like in Saturday morning cartoons. This was the slowest part of the climb and we were going at a snail's pace which was totally OK with me.

We went through the steepest part of the cliffs called the Pearly Gates, and all of a sudden we were on the ridge about one hundred feet from the summit. I couldn't believe I was there. I wish I could express the feelings I was experiencing: jubilation, joy, elation, triumph… there just are not enough words. Everybody was just standing there, looking, talking, and not going to the actual summit. I was very anxious to stand on the top and asked Jeff if I could detach myself from the rope. He gave me the OK, I unhooked myself and I walked the final distance to the peak. I was the first one out of all of us to stand on the summit of Mount Hood, and raised my arms high into the air as I did a complete 360° turn. I took off my pack, sat down, and thought about what a huge success and victory this was for me. I was quite literally in heaven.

My most prized highpointing photograph taken on top of Oregon

Everybody else soon followed and we all congratulated each other on our huge success as they reached the top. All my planning along with Jeff's training and leadership got us to this point. We had some lunch while taking in the views, sharing stories, and taking many photos. Mount St. Helens and Mount Rainier were plainly visible to the north. I stared at Rainier for a long time and thought about those poor people from yesterday. "I will get you another day," I said aloud.

271

It took us eight hours to get from the trailhead to the summit, and now it was time to head back down. We really did make awesome time to the top, and I was extremely proud of all of us; especially myself. We roped up and worked our way back down to The Hog's Back. It was just as slow going down as it was going up.

Once at the Hog's Back, we de-roped and started to have some real fun: We glissaded from The Hog's Back for about a mile sliding the whole way on our butts. It saved a lot of walking and a lot of time. The lower we got, the slushier the snow got. When we were about two-miles from the cars, the snow got so slushy that we couldn't slide any longer. We had to walk the rest of the way and were post-holing up to our knees. This made it very difficult and strenuous on us, but we did eventually make it back to the cars. To our surprise, John and James were in the parking lot welcoming us all back one by one. I told them that I really did wish that they could have been up there with us. They both said, "Next time".

We all went out to dinner that night where five members of the team decided that they were still going to do Rainier the next day. I wished them all the best and we parted ways the next morning. John, James and I took the opportunity to tour the Columbia River Gorge on the Oregon side to kill some time before we had to catch our flight early the next morning. John and James had never been to the state of Washington before, so we crossed a bridge over the Columbia, congratulated each other on the momentous occasion, went back across the bridge, and continued our Oregon tour. We had a great time, but we also couldn't wait to get home to share our stories.

As for the others, they did attempt to climb Rainier that next day. They got about halfway up, but could not make it the rest of the way due to bad weather. They camped just an eyeshot away from where the climbing tragedy had just occurred. A ranger had come down off the peak and told them that the wind was so strong near the top that it had picked him up off his feet and blew him a good distance down the trail. I was so thankful that I made the decision not to climb Rainier, and I still stand behind my decision to this day.

If I was ever in a circumstance where people got seriously hurt or even died during one of my highpointing excursions, I didn't know how I would handle it. Would I continue on with my dream? Would I give up on it all? How would something like that affect my family and friends? How would it ultimately affect me? I really couldn't answer these questions I was asking myself. I was now only five peaks away from accomplishing my highpointing dream, and I hoped that nothing even close to what happened to those unfortunate people on Rainier would ever occur to me. Little did I know that my next climb on Kings Peak would ultimately change my highpointing dream forever.

Chapter 14
- Kings, Part II

This hike was initially planned as a two-day trek, but during some discussion in the car on the way up to Utah's highest mountain, we decided to make this the longest day hike we had ever attempted; 24 miles round trip. My longest prior to this was the 22 mile hike during my fourth trip up Mount Whitney which almost killed me. But I was still in pretty good shape since my Mount Hood climb and was up to the task, as were Mike and Joe.

To get to this mountain, we had to drive through Salt Lake City, into Wyoming, and then back down into Utah through some very beautiful back country. Along the way, we got off the Interstate somewhere in Salt Lake to find a Subway; with huge success I might add. Mike had also brought along a huge bag of unsalted peanuts he bought at Costco, so we're talking a big bag here. We munched on these things all day and into the night during our drive.

It was very cold and dark when we arrived at the trailhead at Henrys Fork Campground. Mike and Joe slept outside under the stars, and I wimped-out and slept in the warm car. Those peanuts gave me the worst gas I had ever experienced in my life and I had to sleep with the windows open so I wouldn't asphyxiate myself. What a great start to my Utah adventure.

Utah Kings Peak
13,528' August 15, 1998

We woke up at 4:30AM and were on the trail by 5:00. It was very dark and we really couldn't see anything without having to use our one flashlight. The trail was very muddy and we ended up stepping in several mud puddles. This wasn't the best way to start a long hike, but we just dealt with it the best we could and continued on. We crossed a meadow that was well over a mile wide and extremely muddy as well. This slowed us up a bit, but we proceeded with our common goal to get to the mountain. We had to get up there and back to the car that same day because we were not prepared to spend the night up there. We brought nothing but food and the clothes on our backs. Flashbacks of how unprepared we were in Virginia crossed my mind a few times, but I knew in my heart that we would get this mountain with no issues.

Our first real milestone we had to obtain was a section of the trail called "Gun Sight Pass," and after hours of hiking, we finally reached this point. I had really studied the maps prior to this climb and had come up with a plan to shave a few miles from the hike as well as not having to drop down into another valley that we would then have to hike back up out of. Mike and Joe both agreed and we proceeded from the pass to hike cross-country along this short cut. It was a very easy way to go and I have never been able to quite figure out why the trail was not just made to go this way in the first place. Because there was no trail, we did have to do a lot of boulder hopping for about a mile, but it was well worth it. There were also plenty of cairns people had built to help guide the way.

Kings Peak silhouetted against a beautiful, blue sky

This mountain was interesting because we had to hike for hours just to get to the base of it at Anderson Pass. Once we reached the base, we still had a little over a mile to hike up to the summit. This was the toughest part of the entire hike because there was no visible trail at all at this point; it was boulder hopping and rock scrambling the rest of the way. There was a small group of people resting along the trail at the base and we stopped to talk with them for a while before we went the final distance. They were mostly women, and as it turned out, there were several of them climbing the mountain as cancer survivors and friends of cancer survivors and victims. I had never experienced something like this before and I thought it was pretty cool to witness.

There was no trail for this last mile, but we could see the top way up ahead of us. Finally seeing the actual peak was all it took to get us that final distance. Also during this final segment to the top, we encountered a woman being escorted down from the summit. Actually, she was being carried down. She was experiencing the worst altitude sickness I had ever seen. I felt very bad for her as I went through the same thing on Mount Whitney during my second attempt with Anna. This woman looked awful and I could see the anguish in her face. Somebody on the top actually radioed down to arrange a rescue. As we neared the top, we saw a ranger on horseback far below coming to her rescue. They met up at the base of the mountain where the ranger put her on the horse and they were off for lower elevations; the only way to rid oneself of this awful affliction.

I was feeling very good and decided that I wanted to be first to the summit again just like on Mount Hood. I made my way past Mike where he told me to pace myself. I did pace myself… at a pace greater than his. I don't think I had ever beaten him to a summit before this day, and it felt great. I was the first to the top and, to be utterly cliché, I felt, "On top of the world." Mike was nowhere in sight at this point. He was down below taking his time. I was experiencing some mild altitude sickness along with a mild headache, but I knew I would be off the mountain soon and everything would be great again. This was also the most crowded peak I had ever visited. There were a ton of people up there; most of them were part of the cancer group down below. They were holding a vigil on the summit for their lost family members and friends. It was very sad, but there were also a lot of smiles up there as well. Soon however, all these smiles would turn to fear.

Mike and Joe were still nowhere in sight so I asked a fellow climber up there to take my usual photo. As soon as my picture was taken, I felt the first drops of hell that would haunt us all the way back to the car which was parked some twelve miles away. I had a strange feeling and this was starting to remind me of my North Dakota fiasco. I knew that it was time to get the hell off the mountain as quickly as possible and I didn't want to wait for Mike or Joe.

It was all of a sudden cold and very windy on what had just been a perfectly clear, warm summer day. Dark clouds filled the sky very quickly and I could see a storm blowing a beautiful veil of snow on the mountains far across the valley to the west of me. It was so dreamlike, almost like a beautiful painting in motion. What worried me was that this painting I was admiring was moving in my direction and I knew we would soon be covered in cold, wet snow.

Sitting on top of my 44th highpoint

Mike showed up just as I was getting ready to leave and asked if I would take his picture. I took the photo and told him that we really should get off the summit. He looked past me at the oncoming storm and immediately agreed. Just then it started snowing on us with a vengeance. It was hard snow, but not hail, and it had very cold rain mixed in with it.

"Where's Joe?" I asked. "We really need to get going and we can't leave without him".

"I don't know, but you're right. Let's just go. If we see him on our way down we'll turn him around".

It was raining and snowing very hard at this point and visibility became very poor. We were about one hundred feet down from the summit when we found Joe fighting his way up the mountain. He was walking very slowly with his hiking stick in one hand, and holding his hood on with the other. He didn't see us until we were practically face to face.

"Joe! We gotta get down the mountain now!" Mike shouted.

"What?!" Replied Joe.

"John and I are heading down! You need to come with us! It's getting dangerous up here!"

"I didn't come all this way not to get to the top! I'm still going! How far is it?!"

"You are close!" I shouted back. "It's only about a hundred feet! Go for it! We'll slow down a bit to let you catch up with us, but we are still heading down! Don't spend too much time up there!"

"Sounds good! I'll catch up to you guys in a few minutes!"

This day would soon turn into the most terror-filled event of my life. I always knew that my sport carried risks, and I had experienced quite a few during my highpointing adventures, but nothing could have prepared me for what was about to happen.

The strange electric buzzing noises started a few minutes into our descent from the summit. I didn't know where the sound was coming from, but it was all around me. Being approximately thirty-five miles from the nearest electrical source, I was very confused and curious as to what could be generating such a noise that seemed to be coming from everywhere. I stopped next to a giant rock wall to take shelter from the elements as I waited for Mike to catch up. I also took this time to try and determine where this strange, annoying sound was coming from. I was staring up the trail, watching for Mike through the snow and rain blowing furiously across the mountain when he finally came around the corner and spotted me standing there.

"Hey John! Do you hear that 'buzzing' noise?!"

"Yeah!" I yelled back through the whipping storm, relieved that I wasn't the only one hearing it, "I was just going to ask you the same question! What do you think it is?!"

"No idea!"

"Well, this is going to sound a little strange", I paused briefly, and then hesitantly added, "But the sound seems like… like it's coming from inside my head!"

Mike gave me an odd look of curiosity and skepticism, and then said, "What? How can that be if I'm hearing it too?"

"I don't know" I said with a puzzled look on my face.

We both talked about it for about a minute more, then he suggested that we get going down the mountain. We had a lot of miles ahead of us and we were burning daylight.

I was wearing a waterproof jacket as well as a baseball cap under the hood. The brim of my cap stuck out beyond the hood to shield my eyes from the non-present sun as well as the driving rain and snow. The more I thought about it, the noise actually seemed to be coming from the brim of my cap. As I was walking, I clasped the brim with my wet, glove covered fingers and the buzzing stopped. I let it go and the buzzing started up again. I stopped and turned back towards Mike.

"Mike!" I shouted. "The buzzing is in my cap!"

"What?!" Mike was way behind me again and couldn't hear me over the weather. I turned away from him to keep my face shielded from the torrential downpour. I kept touching the brim of my cap and letting it go again with the same exact results. I did this quite a few times and actually started to find it a little amusing.

The buzzing then started to intensify and fluctuate in intensity. It was a deep, vibrating buzz that tickled my ears and sounded like several bumble bees on steroids flying around in my skull. A thought started to race through my mind and my wonder immediately switched to concern and fear. I reached out and touched the towering rock wall I was walking along and the buzzing stopped. I removed my hand from the rock and it started back up again. Just then I felt the hair on my arms and on the back of my neck start to tingle. I immediately knew what was about to happen and screamed out at the top of my lungs as I dropped to the ground in absolute terror:

"LIGHTNING!"

Without thinking, I instantly braced myself up against the cold rock wall as I curled my body into a tight ball tucking my head in my arms and shutting my eyes tight. Everything in the following second happened in such slow motion that I was able to discern everything that was going on around me. The intense light as well as the deafening clap of thunder frightened me more than the actual hit I took from the blazing bolt of lightning. It felt as if I had been shot in the arm by a high powered rifle. The pain was intense, but because I was so terrified, I was somehow able to ignore the pain as fast as I noticed it. The brilliant flash of light was so bright it was as if my eyes were wide open. The instantaneous sound of electricity flowing up my right arm, around my shoulders and into the rock next to me was surreal. It was a sound only heard in bad sci-fi movies, but this time it was for real. My immediate thoughts were, Am I OK? Did this really just happen to me? Was I just struck by lightning? Why am I not more hurt? Why am I not dead? Am I dead? The silence was deafening and the Fear and sense of vulnerability was overwhelming. I looked at my arm and couldn't understand why there was no burn mark, or any mark for that matter. Just a dry patch of cloth that slowly got wet again as the rain and snow continued to fall.

After what seemed like an eternity, I began to hear screams and shouts all over the mountain of people calling out to their friends, family, and to total strangers making sure that everybody was OK. All of the different sounds of the weather came back as well. The pounding rain and howling wind made it difficult to hear which is why everybody was shouting. All I could think about was how was I going to get off of this mountain alive and back to the presumed safety of our car.

The last time I saw Mike, he was about 25 feet behind me. I quickly stood up and shouted back to him to make sure he was OK. I will never forget his response: "Did you see that?!"

Did I see that? Was he serious? "Mike! I was hit!"

I was trembling and couldn't tell if it was fear mixed in with some adrenalin, or just the fact that we were standing there in a freezing snow storm. Regardless, Mike didn't notice and just stood there staring at me in bewilderment.

"Mike! I really think we should get the hell out of here! This is a messed up situation and we need to get off this mountain right now!"

"Get off the mountain?! We're going to be up here for a while yet!"

"Why?! Why can't we get going?"

He grabbed me by both arms and started checking me all over for evidence that I was hit; brushing the ice off my jacket, lifting my arms, turning me around. I had nothing to show for it. No burn marks, no holes in my clothing, I wasn't dead, nothing. Because the waterproof jacket I was wearing was covered in rain, snow and Ice, and because I was braced up against the wall, the electricity from the bolt took the shortest path to ground which was through the wetness on my jacket and straight into the rock. If my jacket had been dry when I was hit, I know for sure that I would have died. Mike then turned me around to face him and said, "What about Joe?!"

"Joe! Damn! Where is he?!"

I peered out from under my hood and looked past Mike up the cloud covered mountain. I couldn't see anybody or anything. Joe was still up top somewhere and I started to seriously worry about his fate. There was no way he didn't experience the same thing we just went through and I wondered if we should stay put and wait, or go back up and look for him. Lightning was striking the mountain all around us, and it would only be a matter of time before it decided to turn its fury back in our direction. Every flash of light and rumble of thunder caused me to cower like a frightened cat, and I felt as if our situation was increasingly becoming worse with every passing moment.

So the question remained, What about Joe? After a brief discussion, Mike and I both felt that it would be in our best interest to get down to Anderson Pass as quickly as we possibly could. We both felt that Joe would be OK and that he knew what to do as well as his way back down the trail. When he eventually came down the mountain, he would most definitely find us there waiting for him with open arms. I knew that he was certainly more experienced in this stuff than I was, and I somehow just knew that he was OK up there somewhere.

Mike and I started our scramble down the mountain at a slightly quicker pace than we were used to, but because we were walking downhill stepping on loose, wet stones and boulders, we needed to be extra careful not to slip and possibly make our situation even worse by falling and hurting ourselves.

We had only been walking a few minutes when the buzzing noises started back up again. I started to feel panicky and knew that I could not go through something like that again. I knew for a fact that I would not survive a second strike and franticly started looking for ways to lessen the odds of getting hit again. They say that lightning never strikes twice? That's total crap. It does strike twice, and I knew I was going to be a target again if I didn't start using my head.

We continued down the mountain, gingerly walking along the same rock wall that had earlier been my saving grace. I kept my left arm extended so I was always touching the rock with my fingertips thus keeping myself grounded at all times. I could feel the roughness of the rock through my expensive thermal gloves that continually snagged on the numerous sharp edges. I didn't care; I wasn't going to let go of that rock for anything and gloves can certainly be replaced.

My family teasingly calls me a Rocket Scientist because I am often working in far-away lands for months at a time launching communications satellites into orbit. Because of the industry in which I work, I do understand the physics of electricity. I know how it works, what is does, how dangerous it is, etc. It is because of this knowledge that I instinctively dropped and braced myself up against the wall and why I was now walking with my hand always touching the rock. Electricity looks for the shortest path to ground, and if it was going to strike me for a second time, I wasn't going to let it go through my entire body. I would rather sacrifice my arm, hand and fingers than die of heart failure. The buzzing did eventually stop after what seemed like an eternity, even though it had only been about ten minutes. A sense of relief surged through my body because I knew that I was somewhat safe, at least for the time being.

A short time later, we came across an old man being escorted down the mountain by his grandson. We had seen them twice earlier in the day; once during the climb, and then again up on top about an hour later. In talking with this 80 year old man on the way up, he had revealed to us that he climbed this mountain once a year, every year. I asked why and he answered with a big toothy grin, "Because I love it up here. No other reason." This man had actually become an inspiration to me. I had been feeling exhausted and my motivation was waning by the time we met them on the way up. It had been such a long day with so many hard miles behind us. By the time our brief discussion ended, he had in some way passed some of his limitless supply of energy and enthusiasm to me which gave me the extra boost I needed to get myself to the top. I am never going to forget this man. I will and have always thought of him when I needed that extra shot in the arm to get me that extra mile.

The grandson was now helping his grandfather slide down some large, sharp-edged boulders. This forced Mike and me to stop and wait, as there was no easy way around. They both seemed to be OK but were visibly shaken; you could see it in their eyes and in their actions. Like me, they would cringe at every flash of lightning that never seemed to stop. They looked much like I felt; afraid and vulnerable. It was kind of sad to observe them this way after seeing them so cheerful earlier in the day. They were both now very quiet and serious; the grandson carefully helping his grandfather with every step.

I asked the grandson where they were when the bolt struck. He told us that they had been climbing down the trail and had heard somebody up from them shout out the warning just as his aluminum walking stick started to vibrate and give off a humming noise. He said he threw the stick out in front of him to get rid of it as quickly as possible and it was immediately struck by the lightning bolt just as it left his fingers. He was temporarily blinded and had to sit for a few minutes until his sight came back. His grandfather had been behind him and was shielded from the strike. They both did not understand how they were not hit. I told him that it was me that shouted the warning. They both stopped and turned to me to express their thanks.

Most everyone else we talked to on the way down had similar stories, and most said that they had heard the warning and dove for cover. There were others like me that knew lighting was going to strike but had no time to shout. I of course did not see the bolt, but the way I heard it described by everybody makes me wonder how any of us survived the event. I was wondering how so many people scattered all over the mountain could had been affected by the same bolt. As we walked and talked with others, I was able to piece together a story of what had actually happened up there. I determined that none of us were actually struck by the main bolt, but were actually hit by the smaller fingers of lightning that arc out from the main shaft; small or not, still very dangerous, scary and deadly. I could still not believe how lucky we all were and even questioned myself a couple of times if I were actually dead and now just a wandering ghost talking to other ghosts that did not know that they were dead as well. But because ghosts are not affected by wind, rain, cold and fear, I was quickly snapped out of this goofy delusion.

Mike and I eventually made it down to the base of the mountain where we started our frantic search for Joe. Mike called out to him several times, but his voice echoed off the immense mountain walls and disappeared into the vastness of the valley we were standing in. We stayed put for a long while looking up the mountain in front of us, but Joe was nowhere in sight.

Mike continued calling to him as we started our walk along the base towards the trail that would eventually lead us away from the nightmare. We had not seen Joe for at least a couple hours and were getting quite worried. Mike seemed much more worried than I was and it was really starting to show in his actions and his voice. This was not good. I always considered Mike to be the strong one, the person that would be able to get us out of any situation. We had so many miles of muddy trail to

287

hike and only a few hours of daylight to do it in. We needed to keep our wits intact, especially Mike.

We got to the point on the trail that would now lead us away from the mountain. This is where we decided to stay put until we found Joe. Mike continued calling out to him and asked me to do the same. My voice is the type that does not carry well. I tried calling out to him a couple of times until Mike told me to stop wasting my breath. I don't know how people were able to hear me when I shouted my warning earlier. We started making plans of what we would do if we could not find him before dark when he unexpectedly held is hand up in front of my face and told me to be quiet

"What is it?" I whispered.

"Shhhh... I think I heard something".

"What? Do you hear Joe?"

"Shhhh..."

We stood there in total silence. Nothing could be heard but our breathing as well as the drops of rain falling heavily on our clothing at a slow but steady pace. It sounded much like water hitting an umbrella, which would have actually been nice to have at that particular moment. No other sounds could be heard. Mike called out to him again: long, slow and loud like the little boy calling out to Shane at the end of the movie:

"Joooooooooooooooooe!"

It was a moment later when we both heard a very faint shout from up the mountain somewhere. We both immediately turned our heads in the direction of the call. We couldn't really hear what was being said, but my feeling of desperation immediately changed to joy when we realized that it was Joe! We couldn't see him, but hearing his voice told us that he was safe! Mike called out to him again and again we heard his faint response. You could see it in Mike's face how happy he was as well. He turned to me and gave me a huge smile and bear hug then turned back towards the mountain. We scanned the rocky terrain until

Mike finally spotted him out in the distance walking towards us. We all rushed to greet each other. Mike gave him a huge hug and wouldn't let go. I had never seen Mike so emotional before and Joe had a huge smile on his face as well. They were both so overjoyed and it really showed. That's a sign of true friendship right there.

We stood there for a long while sharing our stories. Joe was amazed that I wasn't more hurt or even killed. He told us that while he was sitting on the summit having his photo taken, he felt what he described to us as two pin pricks of electricity shooting into the top of his head. He knew immediately that lightning was about to strike and dove for cover in some large rocks. He was untouched by the bolt which is amazing since he was at the very top of the mountain and closer to it than anybody else. After the strike he quickly gathered up his belongings and started down the east face of the mountain instead of taking the route Mike and I took. Going down the face was a very treacherous way to go, but in a matter of life and death, who cares? It was the shorter way off the mountain.

As we stood there and talked, the rain started to intensify and the wind started to howl again. It was a sure thing that the weather was going to be a huge factor for us the rest of the day and would definitely be slowing us down considerably. We had a very long hike ahead of us, and decided that it would be in our best interest to get moving. We took the short-cut back to Gun Sight Pass where I got a little ahead of the guys; I couldn't see them on the trail behind me nor could I hear them. After what happened up on the mountain, I didn't like to be separated and alone so I stopped on the trail and turned my back to the blowing, pounding rain. There was absolutely no shelter anywhere, no trees, no rocks, no nothing. Just the ground I was standing on. Other climbers began showing up and stopped to wait for their friends and family as well.

289

The driving rain now became sleet and the wind was strong enough to blow us forward down the trail as if it was trying to tell us all to get off the mountain. I was very lucky I had brought all the proper gear as I was perfectly warm and dry. I just kept my back to the storm and patiently waited as I gazed out into the beautiful meadows we had crossed earlier in the day on our way up. I was still slightly shaken from earlier events and tried not to think about it all too much. As I stared out into the sheer beauty that was laid out in front of me, my mind began to relax and wander back to my climb up Humphrey's Peak the previous month in preparation for this hike.

Even though I was standing there in the freezing rain at the foot of Kings Peak thinking back on that awesome day in Arizona, I could almost feel the warmth of the sun from that past climb as if the sun was actually shining on me at that exact moment. I could see the others sitting around me on the summit eating their lunches and sharing exciting stories of the day's activities. I remembered a strange looking black and yellow bird that landed on a rock next to me as if it was a close, trusting pet. I hand fed it some bread and it thanked me by loudly squawking at me a few times before it flew off. It was at that moment when some guy standing next to me knocked me out of my daydream asking, "Did you hear what happened up there on the mountain a few hours ago? Some people were struck by lightning".

Slightly annoyed, I slowly turned and looked at him square in the eyes and replied, "Yes, I know. I was one of them".

"You were one of them?" he skeptically replied.

"Unfortunately yes, but luckily I am OK".

"Are you the one who shouted out the warning to everybody?"

"Yes. How do you know this?"

The man took a step back, now looking at me with a very serious stare. He then said something to me that I thought was a little strange, "God has a plan for you."

290

"Well, whatever ever that plan is, hopefully it involves getting me off this mountain and safely back home to my family. But seriously, why did you ask me this?"

"I don't know. I just felt that you were the one."

He smiled and we both turned our gazes back out to the meadows that would soon be our next little adventure getting back to our cars.

"We'll all get back OK", he said. "Just hope this rain lets up a little before we head out into those meadows".

"Yeah, no kidding. I've had about enough for the day".

I had been standing there in the storm for a good twenty minutes when Mike and Joe finally caught up with me on the trail. I told them that we should all stay together from now on which they agreed to and we were on our way again. About hour later, we were back in the meadows that were now totally flooded. The rain was still relentless and I could now see flashes of lightning as well as hear thunder way out in the distance, unfortunately in the same direction we were headed.

Using the urban legend "Flash Bang" rule, counting the seconds between the flash of lightning and the bang of thunder, you can tell how far away the lightning is. This is not an exact science, but good enough to be able to determine if the lightning was moving closer or further away from us. All three of us were walking single file spaced about twenty feet apart when all of a sudden I was startled by a very bright flash of light. I counted to myself under my breath so that the others wouldn't hear me, "One 1-thousand, two 1-thousand, three 1-thousand, four, 1-thousand" Boom! There was the thunder and it was about four miles away. Four miles was a good distance, I just hoped it would stay that way. There was another bright flash and I started counting again, "One 1-thousand, two 1-thousand, three 1-thousand" Boom! "Three miles." Then another flash, "One 1-thousand, two 1-thousand" Boom! "Damn!"

Mike was in front of me and heard what I had just said. "What's wrong?" he asked. Then another flash of light, "One 1-thousand, two 1-thousand" Boom! "The lightning is getting closer to us".

"I know. I was hoping you wouldn't notice"

"Wouldn't notice? Are you kidding me?"

Then there was another flash of light followed a second later by a loud crack of thunder. Mike shouted back to Joe and I, "If you feel or hear what you felt and heard on the mountain, shout a warning, throw your pack on the ground and curl up into a ball on top of it!"

"Why?!" I asked.

"Because curling up into a ball on top of your backpack will keep you low and insulate you from the ground!"

That sounded totally logical to me. I loosened my backpack and told the others to do the same just in case. I think the adrenalin pumping through my body up on the mountain as well as my new found vital objective of getting off of the mountain as soon as possible, I never really had much time to think about much of anything else. But now that we were walking though what I dubbed 'Lightning Alley', I was becoming very scared and sick to my stomach. What made matters worse was that there was absolutely no shelter anywhere; no trees, no rocks, no nothing. What a nightmare this was continuing to be. When would it ever end? All we could do was to continue walking down the trail to get us closer to the car that was still at least six miles away. The lighting and thunder never got any closer than a mile, but it was still way too close for comfort. The thunder was always deafening and sounded like huge explosions that would rumble loudly for several seconds. Every flash and clap of thunder sent chills down my spine. I had never felt so tiny and insignificant in my life.

Once we reached the edge of the meadows which meant the safety of our car was only three short miles away, the storm started to let up and it was a huge relief to hear the thunder rumbling in the mountains somewhere way behind us now. Right before we got back to the car, we came to a stream that earlier was a trickle and now was a river from all of the rainfall. Again, I was so very lucky to be wearing all of the proper equipment as I had to walk through this up to my knees and not a drop of water found its way into my boots. We finally made it back to the car just as it was getting too dark to see without our flashlight. Making it back to the car felt so good and I knew that it would soon take us away from all of this. We were totally exhausted and none of us felt like driving. Hiking and climbing all of those miles in one day with rain, snow and lightning thrown in nearly did us in. What a long, rewarding, and awful day it had been. I volunteered to drive the first leg home.

We threw our gear in the car and started the long drive home. I only made it about ten miles before I started to nod-off. I was extremely tired and mentally exhausted. Mike and Joe were already passed out. I quietly pulled the car off the road so I could take a quick nap. Mike immediately woke-up and asked what I was doing. After I told him I just needed twenty minutes he exclaimed, "Hell no! Get in the back seat, I'll drive." That sounded good to me.

After I crawled into the back seat and made myself a comfortable spot to get some sleep, I nestled in and started thinking back on the day's events. Right at that moment, I started seriously thinking about quitting highpointing yet again. I thought back to when I got lost in Virginia, my first failed attempt on Mount Hood, The North Dakota misadventure, the two scary hikes through private property, and now this fiasco. With Kings Peak under my belt, I now had 44 mountains completed with only four to go to complete my dream of climbing all 48 mountains. I just had four more mountains to go. All four of them were beasts in their own way, much more dangerous than the mountain that just tried to kill me earlier in the day:

- Borah Peak in Idaho is a tough climb requiring class four mountain climbing skills while crossing an area called "Chickenout Ridge." It is at this ridge where all of the deaths have occurred on Borah, and it got its name due to the fact that that is where many climbers turn back instead of going the final distance to the peak.
- Granite Peak in Montana is one of the most difficult climbs due to technical climbing, poor weather, and route finding. It is so difficult that it was the last of the 50 state highpoints to ever be climbed. Climbers have to cross an area of the mountain called "Froze to Death Plateau" if that gives any clue as to the conditions up there.
- Granite Peak in Wyoming is usually climbed on a four to six day round-trip. It is considered by mountaineers to be the most difficult state highpoint except for Alaska's Denali and possibly Montana's Granite Peak. This is also the most expensive as it requires pack horses and Native American guides from the Wind River Indian Reservation to get you to the base of the mountain.
- Mount Rainier in Washington. Not much more needs to be said other than what was previously described during my Mount Hood Climb. Even as I write these words, a chill goes through my body.

Part of me said, "You've come too far to quit," while the other part said, "Is your life really worth all of this?" I rationally answer no, but I always end-up planning these damn trips anyway. I kept thinking about that eighty year old man up there. And what about all of the other people that had accomplished this before me? Many children had completed all the highpoints as well. I couldn't let them beat me. There was that voice again, "Is your life really worth all of this?" I seriously had a lot of thinking to do. Some people don't think it should take a lot of thinking. I usually don't listen to them because I am on a quest, or maybe just a little stubborn. I had all of these thoughts going through my mind as I tiredly looked out the window and watched the world go by. I really needed some sleep, so I shut off my brain the best I could and passed-out.

Chapter 15
- Everything Must End

Idaho Borah Peak Attempt # 1

Before my Kings Peak 'adventure of a lifetime', I had already planned out my 45th mountain climb up Borah Peak in Idaho. I was still very shell-shocked from what happened to me in Utah, but I felt obligated to follow through on this next climb since I had already put so much time and effort into the planning of this trip. I also had people lined up to join me; none other than Mike, Joe, and James B. again.

I knew this was going to be a very strenuous climb and I needed to keep myself in shape. To accomplish this, I decided to climb Boundary Peak in Nevada for a second time since it was somewhat close to where I lived and similar in characteristics to Borah. Mike and Joe thought it was a great idea and decided to join me on the climb. My buddy James B. who had just returned with me from his disappointment on Mount Hood was also interested in the climb. Before I knew it, all four of us were piled into my old, rickety RV heading off for the highlands of Nevada.

My 1978 Dodge was only able to squeak-out about six mpg which drove Mike absolutely nuts. Mike was always giving me crap about even owning such a vehicle. But since we were going to have a warm, comfortable place to sleep for the next couple of nights, he let his values temporarily slide for this trip. He said it was his first road trip where instead of figuring out how much time it was between cities, he figured it in gallons of gasoline. I remember passing a road sign stating, "Bishop – 18 Miles."

Mike immediately stated, "Hey! We're three gallons from Bishop!" with a forced smile on his face.

It was already dark when we started up the twelve mile dirt road that would lead us to our camp at the base of the mountain. It was a moonless night and pitch-black outside. Driving along the sheer cliff walls was already making me nervous enough when Mike all of a sudden yelled "LOOK OUT!" This was immediately followed by a huge thud as the whole right rear side of the RV lifted up, and then crashed back down to the ground as everything inside the RV fell on top of us. My heart was pounding as I stopped and turned off the motor. All of us looked at each other as we listened to the strange hissing noise coming from outside.

I had hit a rock the size of a toaster oven and blew out one of my tires. After we assessed the damage, I dug out everything we were going to need to change the tire. I placed it all on the ground next to the RV when at that same exact moment it started to rain on us. I heard a slight giggle behind me and looked back to Mike who immediately broke out into hysterical laughter.

"What is so funny?!"

"This is awesome!" he said.

"What?!" I replied, slightly aggravated.

"This is awesome! Changing a tire in the rain on a muddy dirt road next to a cliff at nine thousand feet in the middle of the night! It doesn't get any better than this."

Mike and his dark sense of humor struck again, but I always loved it. Meanwhile, James was under the motor home trying to jack it up off the ground when I heard him say: "Uh, John? We have a problem."

I looked under the motor home and saw that the jack was sinking into the mud. Being the engineers we all were we immediately went into action to remedy this problem by digging out the jack and setting it on some long strips of wood. As soon we were ready to start jacking up the motor home again, Mike said: "Uh, John? We have a problem."

"What now?!"

The lug nuts holding on the wheel were rusted solid and would not break loose. I looked at Mike and said, "Does any of this remind you of anything?"

"Hmmm, let me think." Mike replied. "Our climb in Virginia? Or North Dakota perhaps?"

"Yep!" I said. "How come it always rains on us whenever things go wrong on our climbs?! Every single time!" We laughed for a bit, and then got back to business.

It took us two hours to change that damn tire. James had to jump up and down on the tire iron to break those lug nuts loose. Every one of them broke loose with a loud "Pop!" Somewhere in the middle of all of this, a truck had pulled up behind us and patiently waited. He had no other option as we were blocking the narrow canyon road. When we were done with the tire, we all piled back into the RV and continued on up to the camp site. We didn't even get close to where we wanted to camp for the night as the road became narrow and impassable due to the size of my motor home. I found a clear, level space to pull onto, cut the motor, and we were all fast asleep in no time.

The RV had bunk beds; Mike took the lower bunk and Joe took the top. It was hilarious listening to Joe curse his way out of and back into his bunk in total darkness whenever he had to use the restroom. We all laughed out loud every time. The next morning when we awoke, Mike announced that he would not be going with us on the climb due to a severe headache he was experiencing. He got these from time to time, and I always felt so bad for him. I can only describe them as migraine, based on how he described them to me.

We left Mike to heal himself and were on our way. I learned from my last climb of Boundary Peak to wear gaiters this time so that my boots wouldn't fill with gravel again. What a painful

299

experience and nuisance that was. Try to imagine hiking in steep, slippery terrain with gravel trapped between the side of your boot and your ankle... Yeah. I was in very good shape for this climb, and was always well ahead of the others during the entire hike. Every once in a while I would stop for a break to let them catch up. We were at about 12,000 feet when I was approaching a ridge to where we would be able to see Boundary Peak for the very first time during the climb. I was about 25 feet from the ridge when I stopped to yell back to the guys to tell them what they were about to see. James who was about one hundred feet down the trail from me yelled up:

"I'll bet you a hundred bucks I can beat you to the ridge!"

"Are you nuts?! I'm only 25 feet away! There is no way you could even come close!"

He immediately dropped his pack started running up towards me. I quickly turned and ran the short distance to the ridge. Being at 12,000 feet with the lack of oxygen and all, I collapsed to my knees and fell flat on my stomach. I was gasping for air like a goldfish that jumped out of his bowl, and my head was pounding and felt as if it was going to pop. Once I was able, I rolled onto my back to see what was keeping James so long. I spotted him down the trail lying on his back staring straight up at the sky holding his head in his hands. He was only about twenty feet from where he dropped his pack. I started laughing so hard that I immediately had to stop when my head felt like it was going to pop again. I yelled down to him holding my head in my hands, "You can keep your money!"

A short time later on that warm afternoon of August 7, 1999, I was able to claim Boundary Peak for a second time. This also meant that I was now ready to conquer Borah Peak in a couple of weeks; or at least I hoped so...

Sitting on top of Nevada for the second time

A couple of weeks later, we were all headed north up Interstate 15 through the hot California and Nevada deserts, through the beautiful state of Utah and then into Idaho. As soon as we crossed the border into Idaho, Mike asked, "Hey John. Did I ever tell you how Idaho got its name?"

Having fell for one of these on several occasions, I immediately replied, "Yes, but I bet James and Joe don't know."

Mike looked over at me and smiled. James and Joe were sitting in the backseat with looks of genuine curiosity across their faces. Mike proceeded to tell his story using his rearview mirror for eye contact. "Well, when the first settlers arrived in a border town not far from here, a man asked what was the name of the land that was laid out beyond the town. A woman working in a brothel thought she heard the man ask, 'Where can I get laid in this town?' She yelled out, 'Mister! I-da-ho!' And that is how Idaho got its name."

The silence from the backseat was deafening until James finally responded with, "Oh... my... god..."

"Yeah," I responded, "You should have him tell you how Connecticut, Minnesota and Canada all got their names as well."

"No thanks," said Joe in a low monotone voice.

When we eventually pulled off the freeway in Blackfoot, Idaho to start our one hundred mile trek across the countryside towards the peak, we found a Subway right at the end of the ramp. We sat down for a meal and I gazed out the window towards the mountains we were going to climb the next morning. I spotted a huge mass of thunderheads way off in the distance hovering in the general direction of Borah Peak. "Damn it!" I thought to myself. Borah Peak was also famous for its lighting strikes, and it looked as if this was going to have to be a consideration now. I decided that it was only right for me to tell the guys that if there was a storm going on up there when we started our climb the next day that I would not be joining them. This of course shocked and upset the others, but I was not going to put myself through what I had just experienced on Kings Peak. No way. Once was enough for any person.

As we drove closer to Borah, the clouds started getting larger and darker, and it began to rain. By the time we made it to the trailhead, it was absolutely dumping on us, and the thunder and lightning was very menacing and nerve-racking. It was getting dark, and our plans to sleep under the stars were dashed by the wind and rain. James decided that he was not going to let a little rain stop him from sleeping outside, so he went outside and started building a shelter to sleep in right next to the car. We all watched out of the warmth of our dry car as James fought with his tarp for fifteen minutes until he gave up and dove back inside the car to escape the elements. It was too funny. Here were four grown men trying to sleep in a mid-sized car that wasn't big enough to even be a little comfortable.

The lightning and thunder lasted all night, and startled me quite a few times. Needless to say, I got very little sleep that dreadful night. As morning approached, the rain had stopped and the clouds had begun to break. I sat there all bundled up in the front passenger seat and watched the clouds very closely for an hour or so before the others woke-up. I wanted to see what they were up to; they did break, but they never left. They clung to the tops and the sides of all the mountains around us. In this part of the country, monsoons are notorious for springing up on you by surprise, and I knew that this is what would happen to us later in the day while we were on the mountain.

I did a lot of thinking and soul searching as I sat there and gazed out the window. I had decided a long time ago after my bout with meningitis that there was nothing more important in my life than my health and my family. I thought back on my predicaments during my previous climbs and noticed they all had a commonality that I just couldn't ignore any longer:

- Mount Hood, Attempt #1 - Fear and anxiety made me quit the climb
- Taum Sauk Mountain - Fear and anxiety almost made me skip the mountain
- Backbone Mountain - Fear while being pursued by the unknown
- Mount Rogers - Fear and anxiety made me quit highpointing altogether
- White Butte - Anxiety over being lost
- Jerimoth Hill – Didn't really talk about it, but there was some fear and anxiety going on while doing something I shouldn't had been doing in the first place
- Kings Peak - Fear and anxiety taken to the next level

Kings Peak... I thought a lot about what had happened to me on Kings Peak.

I planned the trip to Borah not even considering this type of weather, and here I was staring it in the face again. A battle ensued in me to either climb, or not to climb Borah. I went back and forth on why I should and should not have done it. My health and family won the argument each and every time. I was so very lucky on Kings that day. Would I be so lucky this particular day on Borah? Did I want to take a gamble and risk everything? I also knew that if I did not climb Borah that day that my highpointing dream would come to a finality that I wasn't quite sure I wanted to face. I finally knew in my heart what decision was the best one, and this is why I was so frightened to tell the others when they eventually awoke; especially Mike who had done so much with me on these trips and shared in the common dream.

I finally got to a point to where I was good with my decision and continued to wait for the others to awake. I watched other hikers as they left their camps and headed up the mountain, including a Boy Scout troop. And because I was feeling good with my decision, I was able to finally get another thirty minutes of good sleep in before the others finally awoke. Once everybody was 100% awake and ready to get the day started, I told them all to hold up a minute because I had something to say.

They were all a little upset with me after I told them, and tried to talk me into going. I told them that there was absolutely no chance of this happening. I told them to all go without me and that I would wait for them in the car. For some strange reason, they wouldn't even consider going without me; if I wasn't going, then they were not going. I thought this was a bluff or some kind of reverse psychology, but I stood my ground and told them again that I was not going. I told them that they had come all this way and should not let me stop their climb.

They were still very upset with my announcement and were not going to do the climb without me.

Mike suggested that we stay there another night to see how the conditions would be the next day. I told everyone that was fine with me, but if it was still cloudy or raining the next day that I would still not go. Immediately after I said this, Mike started the car and proceeded to drive down the dirt road to the highway that would lead us home. I looked back at the others, but they sat there quietly not saying anything. I told Mike to turn around and go back to the mountain so they could climb it. Mike stopped the car abruptly, looked at me and asked: "Are you going to climb this mountain?"

"No."

He took his foot off the brake, stepped on the accelerator and we were headed for home.

I felt bad about this for a long time, and actually felt as if I had let them all down, but I had to keep reminding myself that my life and my family were most important, and I was not going to do anything to risk losing either. To this day I have never really figured out why they did not do the climb, and they have never told me. In hindsight, I think they knew I was right; that it was too much of a risk. And now that it is all said and done, and speaking from experience, I know I made the right decision that cold, wet morning, and I would do it again in a heartbeat. We did visit Craters of the Moon National Monument on the way back down through Idaho, but after that it was a long quiet ride home. There would be no stopping in Vegas for the all you can eat pancake breakfast this time around.

A short time after my life changing Mount Borah experience, I transferred within my company to another organization where Mike and I couldn't really keep in contact the way we used to. We had worked side-by-side for about twelve years, and it had come to an end. About a year after our struggles on Borah and Kings Peaks, Mike sent me an e-mail stating that we had to plan our next attempt on Borah. I did not reply to him for about a week. I had not really thought much about highpointing during this time, and really needed to think about it seriously before I gave him an answer. I knew in my heart that I wanted nothing more to do with it, and I actually talked to my family and friends about it as well. They all agreed with me that I should give it all up. One of my close friends even told me that I was foolish for even considering it after all that happened. He said that the high altitudes must have fried my brains, and that if I tried it again it would prove to him that I had no brains left at all. I had to agree. I eventually replied to Mike's e-mail stating that I was done with the whole highpointing thing along with my reasons, and I didn't hear back from him again for a very long time. This was a sad period to such a great team that had accomplished so much together. Lucky for me, Mike and I are still very good friends to this very day.

Looking back over my entire highpointing journey, I guess it was my fears and anxiety that eventually came out one of the victors to my story; or better yet, the victorious antagonist. I put up the good fight and was able to persevere by completing 44 of the 48 mountains, but it was my damn fears and anxieties that would not let me finish the final four.

Several years after Idaho, I finally found time to do some research on the topic of anxiety to try and understand it better. I wanted to know exactly what it was and why it affected people the way it did; especially me. I am not going to dwell on the subject as there are plenty of other books out there that already cover this topic in great detail, but the main element that stuck with me is this: The loose definition of anxiety is: *Worry or uneasiness of mind caused by fear of danger,* which absolutely sums it up for me. Every time there was a little fear of danger, or even of the unknown, anxiety would rear its hideous head as it still does from time to time. I do not understand why I have anxiety or where it even came from, but I do know that I do not have it as bad as others and for that I am eternally grateful. But the fact that I even have it at all really does bother me. I have come to the realization that fear, which according to the definition is the main cause of anxiety, is just part of life. It's just how to manage this fear that I still need to figure out and work on.

People often ask me if I will ever complete the remaining four highpoints. As was pointed out previously, these remaining mountains are beasts. Even thinking about climbing any of them causes a slight shortness of breath; which is a side-effect of anxiety! No thank you very much. I guess the only way you would ever find me standing on top of these last four peaks is if I was taken to the summits by helicopter, and even then I don't know if I could do that. Anxiety is a funny thing. It really does mess with your mind, and you are always thinking about everything and anything that could go wrong. In the end, I am just so very fortunate and grateful that I got as far as I did. Who knew that by chasing my highpointing dream that took root at the base of Mount Whitney so long ago, would eventually take me to all these awesome places that I never thought or even dreamed of going? I am truly one lucky person.

48 Mountains

Chapter 16
- Fourteen Years Later

Many years after my highpointing career came to an end, I started a new (much safer) conquest; to visit as many Hard Rock Cafés as I possibly could before I shuffled off this mortal coil. My company sent me to every corner of the planet to launch satellites into space for them, and I took advantage of these trips to visit nearby cities hosting a Hard Rock Café. I also sometimes planned family vacations to where I could visit a Hard Rock or two before coming home. I collected the pins and shot glasses from each café as mementos of my great achievements, and have them proudly displayed in my home office.

It was just about at the same time as I completed this memoir that I was sent away to Florida on company business. There was a ten day period where I only had to work a few hours, and then have the next couple of days off. I decided drive to Destin, FL to get the Hard Rock there on one of those days. I was almost there when I realized I was only about thirty miles from Florida's highpoint. All of a sudden a little voice in my head told me that if I visited Florida's highpoint again, that it would be a great ending to my book... that was already completed.

When I exited the freeway, I had to decide to turn left to Destin, or turn right to Britton Hill. The light was red, so I had a minute to think about it. It was actually starting to get dark, so if I was going to visit Britton Hill, it would have to be now or never. If I skipped Britton Hill and went to Destin, would I end up someday kicking myself in the butt for missing such an opportunity? The light was still red when I looked left towards Destin. The light turned green as I looked right towards Britton

Hill. It was at that exact moment I saw a Subway down the street calling to me. The car behind me honked its horn, and I immediately made the right turn to Subway.

When I got out of the car to get my sandwich, I started chuckling to myself. How perfect was this. I saw the next couple of hours uncontrollably planning itself out in my head, and I just thoughtlessly followed along. I got my sandwich, got back in my car, set the new coordinates in my GPS, and found myself back on top of Florida's highest mountain for the second time in my life on December 30, 2013. I got out of the car, walked the short distance to the marker, and started laughing to myself again; this time out loud. This was so ironic because I knew that I would have to add this to my story, and that my very last highpoint visited would not only be America's lowest, but also very unremarkable as well.

I went back to the car to get my sandwich, walked back to the marker and sat on a nearby bench to enjoy it. I was the only person up there, and couldn't get over how incredibly quiet and peaceful it was. It was a little cold and gray, and just like many of my other highpointing stories, it started to rain. I could hear the raindrops softly hitting the canopy of leaves above with such clarity as it protected me from getting wet. Once I finished my sandwich, I walked over to the same trash can that had a fury resident the last time I was there. I slowly peered into the can as if he would still be there this many years later. I decided that this moment just had to be shared with one of my best friends in the world. I took out my phone and gave Mike a call. He did not answer, but I left him a message of where I was and what I was doing that probably had him laughing out loud as well. I am so glad I took that right-hand turn that evening. Just before I got back in the car to go to Destin, I took a moment to look around and to let it all soak in. I also took my very first selfie that evening with the highpoint prominently displayed in the background. Unfortunately my phone broke before I could retrieve the photo which would have ended up being placed right about here. I often think back to what a great moment that was.

Just like what I had just accomplished in Florida, I still keep my highpointing somewhat alive by revisiting highpoints if I happen to be in the general area. I will continue to do this whenever possible for the rest of my days... the easy ones at least. I'll just wave at the hard ones as I drive safely by. I have lunch with Mike quite often at our local Subway where we always reflect on our past climbs, share our stories, and have good laughs. We really did have a great time during our travels, there is no doubt about that at all. Mike's highpointing total stands at 45 peaks completed. I recently asked him if he ever thought about completing his final three to which he responded, "Only if you do them with me." My immediate response was, "Nope. I'm done", and that's where it all stands.

To verify that I had captured every last mountain climbing detail for this memoir, I recently located my trusty guidebook to review my notes for the very last time. It was at the exact moment when I spotted the book sitting on a dusty shelf in my office that it dawned on me that I was still keeping it in the same exact Ziploc bag that had come open and allowed everything to spill out onto the frozen summit of Taum Sauk Mountain in Missouri that one frozen night so many years ago. I took the bag and its contents off the shelf and dusted it off before I opened it. It was at that moment where I thought I could hear Mike in the back of my mind saying, "Hey John! Why do you keep your book in a Ziploc bag? Is it to keep it dry?! How's it goin' eh!? HA HA HA!!!"

This brought a huge smile to my face. I swear I will never be able to live that one down, even when he is not around.

48 Mountains

My chronological list of peaks completed:

#	State	Peak	Date	#	State	Peak	Date
1	Arizona	Humphreys Peak	6/23/1991	25	Minnesota	Eagle Mtn	6/5/1996
2	California	Mount Whitney	7/14/1991	26	North Dakota	White Butte	6/6/1996
3	Nevada	Boundary Peak	8/25/1991	27	Texas	Guadalupe Peak	8/30/1996
4	Georgia	Brasstown Bald	9/10/1992	28	Nebraska	Panorama Point	8/31/1996
5	Tennessee	Clingmans Dome	9/10/1992	29	Florida	Britton Hill	12/28/1996
6	Colorado	Mount Elbert	9/4/1993	30	Alabama	Cheaha Mtn	12/28/1996
7	Missouri	Taum Sauk Mtn	3/4/1995	31	Mississippi	Woodall Mtn	12/29/1996
8	Indiana	Hoosier Hill	3/4/1995	32	Delaware	Ebright	6/24/1997
9	Ohio	Campbell Hill	3/4/1995	33	Massachusetts	Mount Greylock	6/26/1997
10	Pennsylvania	Mount Davis	3/4/1995	34	New York	Mount Marcy	6/27/1997
11	Maryland	Backbone Mountain.	3/4/1995	35	Vermont	Mount Mansfield	6/27/1997
12	West Virginia	Spruce Knob	3/5/1995	36	New Jersey	High Point	6/28/1997
13	Virginia	Mount Rogers	3/5/1995	37	Connecticut	Mount Frissell	6/28/1997
14	Kentucky	Black Mountain	3/5/1995	38	Rhode Island	Jerimoth Hill	6/28/1997
15	North Carolina	Mount Mitchell	3/6/1995	39	Maine	Mount Katahdin	6/29/1997
16	South Carolina	Sassafras Mtn	3/6/1995	40	New Hampshire	Mount Washington	6/30/1997
17	Kansas	Mount Sunflower	6/1/1996	41	New Mexico	Wheeler Peak	8/15/1997
18	Oklahoma	Black Mesa	6/1/1996	42	South Dakota	Harney Peak	8/16/1997
19	Louisiana	Driskill Mtn.	6/3/1996	43	Oregon	Mount Hood	6/12/1998
20	Arkansas	Magazine Mtn	6/3/1996	44	Utah	Kings Peak	8/15/1998
21	Iowa	Sterler Farm	6/3/1996	45	--	--	--
22	Illinois	Charles Mound	6/4/1996	46	--	--	--
23	Wisconsin	Timms Hill	6/4/1996	47	--	--	--
24	Michigan	Mount Arvon	6/4/1996	48	--	--	--

48 Mountains

America's Highpoints:

State	Highpoint	Elevation	State	Highpoint	Elevation
Alabama	Cheaha Mtn.	2,407'	Montana	Granite Peak	12,799'
Alaska	Mount McKinley	20,320'	Nebraska	Panorama Point	5,424'
Arizona	Humphreys Peak	12,633'	Nevada	Boundary Peak	13,143'
Arkansas	Magazine Mtn	2,753'	New Hampshire	Mount Washington	6,288'
California	Mount Whitney	14,494'	New Jersey	High Point	1,803'
Colorado	Mount Elbert	14,433'	New Mexico	Wheeler Peak	13,161'
Connecticut	Mount Frissell	2,380'	New York	Mount Marcy	5,344'
Delaware	Ebright	442'	North Carolina	Mount Mitchell	6,684'
Florida	Britton Hill	345'	North Dakota	White Butte	3,506'
Georgia	Brasstown Bald	4,784'	Ohio	Campbell Hill	1,550'
Hawaii	Mauna Kea	13,796'	Oklahoma	Black Mesa	4,973'
Idaho	Borah Peak	12,662'	Oregon	Mount Hood	11,239'
Illinois	Charles Mound	1,235'	Pennsylvania	Mount Davis	3,213'
Indiana	Hoosier Hill	1,257'	Rhode Island	Jerimoth Hill	812'
Iowa	Sterler Farm	1,670'	South Carolina	Sassafras Mtn	3,560'
Kansas	Mount Sunflower	4,039'	South Dakota	Harney Peak	7,242'
Kentucky	Black Mountain	4,145'	Tennessee	Clingmans Dome	6,643'
Louisiana	Driskill Mtn.	535'	Texas	Guadalupe Peak	8,749'
Maine	Mount Katahdin	5,267'	Utah	Kings Peak	13,528'
Maryland	Backbone Mtn.	3,360'	Vermont	Mount Mansfield	4,393'
Massachusetts	Mount Greylock	3,491'	Virginia	Mount Rogers	5,729'
Michigan	Mount Arvon	1,979'	Washington	Mount Rainier	14,410'
Minnesota	Eagle Mtn.	2,301'	West Virginia	Spruce Knob	4,863'
Mississippi	Woodall Mtn.	806'	Wisconsin	Timms Hill	1,951'

 For more photos, stories and fun, please visit me on facebook: 48 Mountains

Follow me on twitter @johnnywhite1963

Find my book on amazon.com

FURTHER INFORMATION:

www.highpointers.org

Highpoints of the United States, by Don W. Holmes

Made in the USA
Coppell, TX
15 March 2021